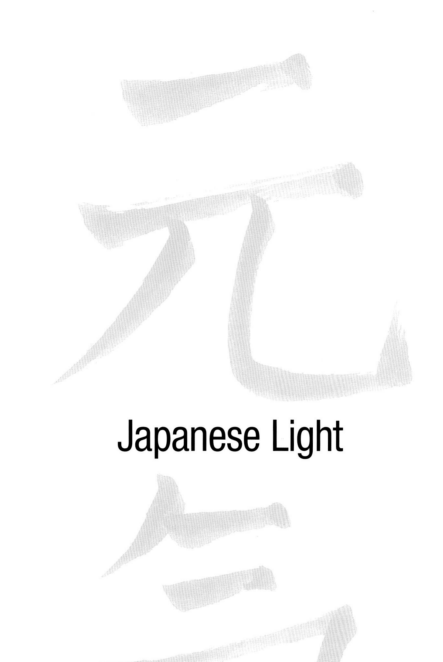

Japanese Light

Kimiko Barber

Japanese Light

photography by Jan Baldwin

To Stephen, my husband, lover, father of our boys, Maxi, Frederick and Dominic,
advisor and most of all, best friend

To Mrs Junko Ohtaki and her young doctor son, Yuhei Ohtaki

All recipes serve 4, unless otherwise stated

LONDON, NEW YORK, MUNICH, MELBOURNE, AND DELHI

First published in the Uinted States by
DK Publishing
375 Hudson Street
New York, New York 10014
Discover more at www.dk.com

First published in Great Britain by
Kyle Cathie Limited
122 Arlington Road, London NW1 7HP
general.enquiries@kyle-cathie.com
www.kylecathie.com

© 2006 by Kimiko Barber
Design © 2006 by Kyle Cathie Limited
Photographs © 2006 Jan Baldwin

DK Books are available at special discounts for bulk purchases for sales promotions, premiums, fund-raising,
or educational use. For details contact DK Publishing Special Markets, 375 Hudson Street, New York, New York
10014 or SpecialSales@dk.com.

Edited by Sophie Allen
Art direction and design by Vanessa Courtier
Photography by Jan Baldwin
Home economy by Linda Tubby and Louise Mackaness (front cover, pp21, 27, 127, 135, 142)
Styling by Wei Tang
Proofreading by Ruth Baldwin
US recipes edited by Peggy Fallon
Production by Sha Huxtable and Alice Holloway

A CIP catalog record for this book is available from the Library of Congress.
ISBN (13-digit) 978-0-7566-2603-7

Colour Reproduction by Colourscan Pty Limited
Printed in China by C&C Offset

Contents

Introduction

I love food. Above all, I am a passionate home cook; I love sharing the food I've cooked with my family and friends. I believe that the food I love and grew up with has kept us all happy and healthy. In this book I want to extend my passion for Japanese home cooking to you to share with your own family and friends.

Every culture has its own unique history of food and cooking, and Japanese cuisine is no exception—it has a long, deep-rooted and rich history. A nation's cuisine occupies a more important position than is often perceived but, above all, it has a profound effect on the nation's health. Today, more than at any other time in recent history, there is a heightened awareness of food and health. Hardly a week passes by without another finding or warning, with bewildering, not to mention downright confusing, claims and counterclaims about what to eat, what not to eat, and how to eat. Furthermore there is no end to new fashionable "diets", adding to our fear and confusion. We are bombarded with "information" on food. All this is turning the pleasure of eating into something we feel guilty about. I want to stop that and take you back to the simple pleasure of home cooking and home entertaining because I know that healthy eating starts at home.

I was born in the mid 1950's in Kobe, Japan, where I grew up until I left for England in the early '70's. I was fifteen when I arrived at boarding school. I loved my school but the food made me very homesick. My least favorite dishes were rice pudding and over-cooked vegetables that had lost their goodness, nutrition, taste, texture, colors, and flavors; in other words, their integrity. How I longed for my mother's and grandmothers' cooking—authentic Japanese home food. During my first term at school, I lost so much weight my mother did not recognize me when I met her at the Tokyo airport. I had become disenchanted with school food and had developed an unhealthy attitude toward food. Thank goodness, I returned home to my mother and three grand-mothers who were all passionate cooks. During that Christmas and New Year holiday, I went back into their kitchens and we cooked together. Even simple tasks like washing and chopping seasonal vegetables felt worthwhile and deeply satisfying. The happy ending to this story is that I regained my love of food and my passion for good home cooking that has never left me since.

It gives me great pleasure to see that there are over 100 Japanese restaurants in London alone and many more are thriving all over Britain today. Many chefs, both Japanese and non-Japanese, stretching from New York to Sidney, are creating exciting cutting-edge food that puts Japanese cuisine in the mainstream of world cuisine. It fills me with even greater pleasure to see that locals are filling the restaurants once kept in business by homesick Japanese businessmen and tourists. Many Japanese ingredients, formerly regarded as strange and hard to find, are now readily available on supermarket shelves. Furthermore, increasing numbers of British farmers are growing Asian vegetables, that are becoming available in supermarkets.

Thirty years ago, when I first arrived in England as a teenager, it was beyond my wildest dreams to see packed sushi lunch boxes on sale next to sandwiches on supermarket shelves. How things have changed. However, compared to more "established" Asian cuisines such as Chinese and Indian, Japanese food is still a relatively new arrival and is yet to make itself at home in most Western home kitchens. Japanese food to many people is still shrouded in mystery and seen as a difficult style of cooking. It is my mission to dispel these mysteries and bring Japanese food into everyone's home kitchen. It is a simple fact that restaurant chefs and home cooks are catering for two different audiences—chefs are expected to excel, they are trained, have access to well-equipped professional kitchens with staff and a wide range of ingredients; home cooks aim to nourish their family and friends and keep them well fed, happy, and healthy.

As palates become more adventurous and sophisticated, informed diners are seeking food that is not only tasty but also healthy. They want food that is low fat, low cholesterol, less dependent on meat and dairy products with more emphasis on vegetables and fish. In fact, the Japanese way of eating is exactly how modern Westerners are trying to eat today.

It is well known that Japanese men and women have the longest life expectancy in the world. Japan has the lowest incidence of heart-related disease among developed nations. Obesity is almost unheard of yet (I say "yet" because Japanese eating habits are rapidly changing) and, with the exception of Sumo wrestlers, it is hard to spot a fat person. Although the evidence is still tentative, there are a number of studies that link the low incidence of menopausal symptoms among Japanese women with a soy protein-based diet. Breast cancer is also rare. I am not suggesting that you should radically change your diet to Japanese food alone, but I invite you to explore the Japanese way of cooking and eating because it is delicious, healthy, and surprisingly easy.

The philosophy of Japanese cooking

The Japanese word *washoku* is used to distinguish Japanese food from foreign-inspired food, known as *yoshoku*. It is no coincidence that the character *wa* represents peace, harmony, and softness. The philosophy of *washoku* is encapsulated in the five principles—five colors, five tastes, five ways of cooking, five senses, and five outlooks. The first three principles cover the practical elements of meal preparation, while the fourth principle defines the sensual elements of food; that is, that food must appeal to all five senses, not just taste and smell. The final principle is more spiritual; it requires us to respect and appreciate human endeavor and the forces of nature that provide for us.

The five colors, *go shiki*, preaches that every meal should have five colors: white, red, yellow, green, and black (including dark colors like purple and brown) to achieve a nutritious diet.

The five tastes, *go mi*, means that a meal should contain a harmonious balance of saltiness, sourness, sweetness, bitterness and *umami* to stimulate, but never to overwhelm, the palate.

The five cooking methods, *go hoo*, urges cooks to use a variety of different ways of preparing foods: simmering, grilling, and steaming being the most common as well as frying and

aemono–the best translation is cooked salads.

The five senses, *go kan*, must be stimulated, so not only taste, but smell, sight, sound and touch. In fact, taste is the last element of the five senses, while sight, or a visually pleasing presentation, is an important part of a meal. We have a saying in Japanese that "we eat with our eyes."

The five outlooks, *go kan mon*, are rules concerned with the partaking of food, and stem from Buddhism, especially the demanding Zen sect where monks observe a strict vegetarian diet of *shojin ryori*. In Zen Buddhism the preparation and eating of food are an important part of the training. First, they instruct us to respect and be grateful for the efforts of all those who contributed to growing and preparing the food. Second, we must do good deeds worthy of receiving food. Third, we must come to the table in peace. Fourth, we should eat food for spiritual nourishment as well as physical well-being. Fifth, we must be earnest in our struggle to attain spiritual enlightenment.

Umami is the fifth sense of taste after salty, sour, sweet, and bitter. The flavor of food is determined by a number of different factors including taste, smell, color, texture, temperature, overall appearance, and our memory as well as by physiological or psychological condition. We all have tasted it and know it but do not know exactly how to put it into words. There is no direct translation in English but in Japanese it is called *umami*, which literally means deliciousness. Umami itself is a subtle savory taste imparted by glutamate and ribonucleotide, including inosinate and guanylate, that occur naturally in many foods such as meat, fish, vegetables, and dairy products. A Japanese professor, Kikunae Ikeda, discovered it in 1907. He knew that there is a taste that is common to mushrooms, tomatoes, cheese, and meat but that is not one of the four well-known tastes. He developed a method of extracting umami by using a large quantity of konbu (kelp seaweed) broth. He managed to extract crystals of glutamate acid, an amino acid that is a building block of protein with a flavor unlike that of the other four tastes. Four ounces of dried konbu contains about 1g of umami.

Echoing the four seasons

In Japan, the five principles are bound up with nature, they include both indigenous Shinto belief and Buddhism and have evolved into a widely encompassing, deeply integrated culinary culture. I often struggle to find an exact word in English to describe Japanese cuisine; in Japanese it is best summed up by the word *shun*, a point in time when a particular food is at its best in taste and flavor. *Shun* can last for several weeks or even months—or it can be a fleeting moment. Although nowadays it is possible to buy almost any ingredient at any time of year, Japanese cuisine, more than any other, respects and appreciates seasonal cycles and other rhythms of nature. And so both professional and home cooks try to echo nature's way of providing us food. Vegetables and fish have their own *shun* when they taste best and are often the most economical. As you would expect, cooking methods and presentation should also reflect the four seasons.

Alphabet of Japanese seasoning

The Japanese alphabet is made up of a series of consonants followed by vowels. For example, the way to express the "s" characters is *sa, shi, su, se, so*. This third line of our 51 member syllabary also happens to relate to the seasonings used in Japanese cooking. The text below shows the exact order in which seasonings are applied to dishes, based on scientifically proven logic. The principle is that bigger particles, such as those of sugar, cannot penetrate foods when obstructed by smaller particles, such as those of salt. So the following seasonings should always be used in the correct sequence, as shown below:

Sa stands for *sato*, which is sugar and sake. Sugar is widely used in marinades and sauces. Sake is used to soften an ingredient or to rid it of odors.

Shi stands for *shio*, which is salt. If salt is applied too early, it tightens the cell structure of an ingredient and makes it more difficult to cook, so it must be added at the correct time.

Su stands for the same-sounding word *su*, which is vinegar. Vinegar evaporates when heated and loses its flavor, so it is vital that it is not added at too early or too late a stage of cooking.

Se stands for *seuyu* or *shoyu*, which is soy sauce. Soy sauce is one of the most important seasoning ingredients of Japanese cuisine. It is added near the end of cooking and is also used for dipping to preserve its unique taste, flavor, and aroma.

So stands for miso. Like soy sauce, this is used to impart added flavor to many dishes.

If all these sound difficult and strange notions to grasp, there is no need to be disheartened, because most young Japanese today would struggle to articulate the *washoku* philosophy, let alone describe the set of five principles. Perhaps they do not discuss the guidelines for preparing a nutritiously well-balanced, aesthetically pleasing meal. Yet, when it comes to choosing items from a restaurant menu, selecting ready-prepared food from deli counters, or buying prepared food from a supermarket only to take it home and reheat in a microwave, most Japanese people, by instinct, employ the five principles to achieve a culinary harmony. It is in our blood.

Selecting ingredients at their best, buying locally available food from both the land and the sea, engaging all the five senses, using a collage of colors, using different methods of cooking, the presenting and serving—the *washoku* approach to cooking provides a cook with the opportunity to be creative in every sense, to satisfy his or her own aesthetic yearnings while providing nourishment and sensory pleasure to family and friends. With this book, I hereby extend my invitation to explore Japanese home cooking.

Japanese pantry

Bonito fish flakes—*katsuo bushi*
Together with konbu (kelp seaweed), this is one of the essential components of dashi—Japanese broth. Traditionally rock-hard, dried bonito fish was shaved just before use, but today ready-shaved flakes available in plastic bags are most commonly used for preparing both dashi and for garnishing.

Potato starch—*katakuri-ko*
Originally the flour was made of the dried root of *Erythronium japonicum*—dogtooth violet, a perennial plant, that belongs to the lily family. Because of this plant's scarcity, today *katakuri-ko* is mostly made of potato flour and is used as a thickening agent and for coating food before frying. Regular cornstarch is a fine substitute.

Japanese green horseradish—*wasabi*
Wasabi is a perennial aquatic plant. Outside Japan it comes most commonly in paste or powder forms. It is used as a condiment and seasoning.

Japanese pepper—*sansho*
Sansho is a low-growing, prickly, deciduous bush that belongs to the tangerine family. Almost every part of the tree is used for home-remedies, garnishing, and seasoning. Sansho powder, which is made of the ground seedpods, is available in small bottles and has a refreshing peppery flavor and aroma.

Kelp seaweed—*konbu*
The most important seaweed used in Japanese cooking this is an essential ingredient for making dashi broth. Sold in packets, it has a dark green-black color, often with whitish patches from dried sea salt. Wipe it clean with a damp cloth but do not soak before using, unless stated.

Noodles
In this book three basic types of noodles are used.

Udon noodles, made of white flour, come in various widths and in either flat or thick strands. They are sold either dried or semi-cooked in vacuum packs.

Somen noodles are also made of wheat, but are very fine and sold in dried form.

Soba noodles are made of buckwheat flour and commonly light or medium brown. The green variety contains powdered green tea. Both varieties are sold in dried form.

Japanese seven-spice seasoning—*shichimi togarashi*

A mixture of several different spices and flavorings, containing sansho, ground red chiles, hemp seeds, dried tangerine peel, ground nori, black and white sesame seeds, and white poppy seeds. All are sold in small bottles in Japanese food stores.

Sesame seeds—*goma*

Both black and white sesame seeds, the latter more common, are used in Japanese cooking for seasoning and garnishing. White sesame seeds are toasted and ground to make a paste. You can buy them already toasted from Japanese food stores. Middle Eastern tahini or smooth peanut butter are good substitutes.

Dried shiitake mushrooms

Shiitake are Japan's most popular mushrooms. The dried variety has a stronger taste and aroma and is used as a flavoring ingredient for many dishes.

Pickled ginger—*gari* or *beni shoga*

Gari is a pale pink pickled ginger used for sushi and as a palate cleanser. It is sold in jars or plastic bags. Bright red beni shoga is used for garnishing.

Pickled plums—*umeboshi*

Salty pickled plums are a dull red color and have a fruity fragrance. They are a popular accompaniment for plain boiled rice as they prevent the rice from spoiling. They should be refrigerated after opening.

Yuzu

This is a Japanese citrus fruit that resembles a tangerine. Its peel and juice are both highly prized and used as seasoning ingredients. It has a refreshing minty taste and pleasant aroma. The juice is available in bottles from Japanese food stores.

Essential seasonings

These five seasoning ingredients provide essential Japanese tastes and flavors. I strongly suggest you try all of them, as most can be found at well-stocked supermarkets.

Soy sauce
Soy sauce is undisputedly the most famous and most widely used seasoning in Japanese cooking. It is made of fermented soya beans, wheat, salt, and water. It has a pleasant nutty aroma with a slightly sweet taste. Outside Japan, you are likely to come across three varieties: dark, light, and tamari. The dark variety is the most versatile and popular. It is used for marinating, dressing, cooking, and dipping. If you are buying just one variety, choose this one. Light soy sauce is surprizingly saltier than the dark and is used mainly in cooking where the intention is not to discolor the ingredients. Tamari in the strict sense should be made without wheat; however, as the term is used loosely by manufacturers nowadays you should read the label carefully if you cannot tolerate wheat products. Tamari is slightly thicker and sweeter in taste than dark soy sauce and is mainly used for dipping.

Miso
Miso paste and soy sauce are the two most important seasoning ingredients in Japanese cooking and they share the same origin (fermented soya beans), though miso is the "older brother" of the two. Miso may contain a variety of grains, including barley and wheat, while the most popular type consists of soya beans mixed with rice culture. Miso comes in a range of colors from light cream shiro miso to near-black haccho miso. In general, the lighter the color of miso paste, the less salty in taste. My suggestion in choosing miso is to start with a medium-colored variety (a shade similar to milk chocolate) and then experiment with lighter and darker types, blending them to suit your taste. Miso is a very healthy food, packed with vitamin E and minerals, and offers easily digestible protein—soya protein converted into amino acid. Miso lowers

cholesterol, helps reduce blood pressure, and is anticarcinogenic. The easiest way to use it is to dilute it with dashi broth to make soup or season simmered dishes. It makes an excellent marinade, good dressings, and a wide range of sauces and dips.

Rice vinegar

Japanese rice vinegar-making developed during the mid-seventeenth century with the fast-growing sake brewing industry. Rice vinegar is a light bronze color, has a pleasant aroma and is mildly sour but not as sharp as wine vinegar or malt vinegar. One of the hardest working ingredients in the Japanese kitchen, it sterilizes, preserves, and acts as a natural antiseptic; it is also used to neutralize fishy odors, reduce saltiness, and tenderize meat. It refreshes the color of cooked vegetables and a small amount added during cooking highlights the flavor of many simmered dishes. Japanese rice vinegar is increasingly easy to find, but cider vinegar makes a good substitute when necessary.

Sake

Sake is Japan's most traditional alcoholic beverage. Although it has long since lost its popularity as a mealtime drink to beer and, more recently, wine, its culinary and cultural importance still remains. As a seasoning ingredient, sake adds flavor and depth to many dishes. It is also used to preserve and marinate, and to neutralize the strong odors of fish and meat.

Mirin

Mirin is a sweet sake used for cooking. It is a light amber-colored liquid with a slightly syrupy consistency and a mild sake aroma. Mirin is used to add sweetness and a glossy shine to foods. Out of the five essential seasoning ingredients, mirin is the least known and perhaps the most difficult to find—sake and sugar make a reasonable substitute, at the ratio of 1 teaspoon of sugar to 1 teaspoon of sake.

Essential utensils

About knives

The most important cooking utensil in the Japanese kitchen is a knife. A Japanese chef's knife is as precious to him as swords are to a samurai warrior. The spirit of the ancient craft of Japanese sword-making lives on, only it is now used to forge kitchen knives made of superior-quality carbon steel. Carbon-steel knives require more care and attention than other types in order to maintain their hair-splitting sharpness. They should be sharpened regularly by hand with a whetstone, but never with a steel knife sharpener or grinding wheel. For a home cook, I suggest buying one stainless-steel kitchen knife that fits well in your hand, and to keep it sharp and well-maintained. You are more likely to injure yourself with a blunt knife, as slicing and chopping require more effort. Do not put your knife in the dishwasher, but wash it by hand and dry it properly before storing. Do not store it in a drawer where other kitchen utensils are kept, as the blade may get damaged. If you have a knife block, turn the knife on its back (dull edge) to slide it in. In other words, try to minimize the blade coming into contact with any hard objects other than food. In Japanese cuisine, preparation, especially cutting, is as important a stage as the actual cooking. Using a sharp knife makes it a more pleasurable experience.

Cooking chopsticks

These chopsticks are longer than the kind used for eating, and are used for both cooking and serving. I personally cannot cook without them in my hand—they are like an extension of my fingers. But if you are not accustomed to using chopsticks, use tongs or a wooden spoon instead.

Japanese pestle and mortar

After my kitchen knives, *suribachi* and *surikogi* are the second hardest-working utensils in my kitchen. They are used for grinding or blending ingredients like miso pastes. A Japanese mortar has a ridged interior to facilitate grinding.

Bamboo rolling mat

This is used to roll Japanese omelets or sushi rolls. It is also used for rolling and squeezing excess water from boiled spinach and other vegetables.

Earthenware casserole

This is used for the wide range of hotpot dishes that are cooked at the table, and for cooking rice. It reliably spreads the heat gently and evenly. There are myriad designs, shapes, and sizes of *do-nabe* to suite the wide range of hotpot dishes. A fondue pot or cast-iron casserole dish makes a good substitute.

Grater

As well as the universal flat or box grater, there is another uniquely Japanese type: a grater that sits on its own shallow dish to collect both the juice and the grated vegetable.

Cutting vegetables

Food preparation is considered a fine art form in Japanese cuisine. As cutting the vegetables plays an important part in this, numerous methods have developed. According to each dish and its cooking method, a cook selects the most appropriate way of cutting the ingredient to ensure that the result will be both visually pleasing and easy to eat with chopsticks. Here are a few of the basic cuts used for preparation and presentation.

Cutting off skin

Round slices

Matchstick-sized pieces

Rolling cuts

Gingko-leaf slices

Shavings

Angled slices

Threads

Dashi—the basic flavor

The classic Japanese dashi broth made of seaweed and dried fish flakes takes only 15 minutes to make. It is so simple. So why dedicate a special section to a mere broth, you ask? Because dashi is more than just broth for soups and stews. In the context of Japanese cooking, it provides the backbone to the entire cuisine—it is the basis of flavor. Dashi gives a subtle undertone to soups; simmered, steamed, or stewed dishes; salads; dipping sauces; rice and noodles; and wholesome hotpots—it is used everywhere. Once you have mastered the basics of dashi-making, you have laid the foundations of Japanese cooking and the rest will follow.

There are many dashi recipes using varied ingredients and often involving rather convoluted preparations, but there are only three basic dashi broths you need to know.

Vegetarian dashi

This is a subtle vegetarian dashi using konbu and dried shiitake mushrooms.

2 postcard-sized pieces of konbu
  (kelp seaweed)
3 dried shiitake mushrooms
4 cups water

Soak the konbu and shiitake mushrooms in the water for 1 hour before placing over low/moderate heat. Slowly bring the water to a gentle boil, but do not let it come to a full boil. Remove the konbu pieces when they begin to float to the surface. Increase the heat and boil rapidly for 2 minutes; then turn off the heat. Let the liquid cool to room temperature before removing the shiitake mushrooms. This will keep for 2–3 days in the refrigerator.

Mizu dashi— "cheater's version"

A good cook uses her/his time wisely and plans ahead. And how better to make flavorsome dashi broth than while you sleep? Although this is called the "cheater's version" you shouldn't feel guilty, because this is how millions of Japanese housewives organize their family meals for the following day.

8 cups warm water
1 postcard-sized piece of konbu
  (kelp seaweed)
3 dried shiitake mushrooms
1/4 ounces dried bonito flakes

Put all the ingredients in a heat-resistant glass jar. Let sit overnight to steep. The bonito flakes will settle to the bottom, but strain before using. This will keep for up to 3 days in the refrigerator.

Number one dashi broth

This is the most popular variety of dashi. In Japanese it is described as "an extracted juice" and I think it is an apt interpretation. Japan is a series of islands surrounded by sea, so it is not surprising that the main building block of its cuisine is made with two marine ingredients: konbu (kelp seaweed) and bonito fish flakes. Good dashi is delicious enough to eat on its own— it is fragrant and subtle yet never fails to ignite a pilot light in me to want to start cooking! The smell of dashi drifting from the kitchen always reminds me of my mother and grandmother's food preparation. I have tried and tested many different ways of making the number one dashi and have come up with this method. It is not the quickest, but it is one of the easiest and the most reliable.

1 postcard-sized piece of konbu
(kelp seaweed)
4 1/2 cups water
3/4 ounces dried bonito flakes
(roughly a handful)

In a saucepan, soak the konbu in 4 cups of water for 1 hour (or at least 30 minutes) before placing over moderate heat. (If the konbu has soaked for less than 1 hour, cook over low heat to allow more time for its flavor to infuse the water.)

Take out the konbu when it begins to float to the surface and a few small bubbles appear at the edge of the saucepan. Pour in 1/2 cup of cold water followed by the bonito flakes. Turn up the heat slightly and cook until the liquid returns to a gentle boil, but do not let it come to a full boil; turn off the heat. Let the bonito flakes settle to the bottom and strain the dashi through a fine sieve lined with a piece of paper towel.

Cook's tip

Although it requires a little advance planning to soak the konbu, the actual cooking takes less than 15 minutes. The result is well worth the effort and indisputably superior to store-bought instant dashi granules that are too salty and often contain monosodium glutamate. I recommend using dashi broth the same day it is made.

soups

Soup occupies a unique position in Japanese cuisine. It is the only dish that appears twice in a meal. At elaborate kaiseki meals consisting of seven, eleven, or even fifteen courses, two varieties of soup are served, at the beginning and end of the meal. To whet your appetite a bowl of delicate clear soup appears at the beginning, while a flavorsome miso soup is served with a bowl of rice and pickles to signal the meal's end. It is said that the culinary skills of a chef are judged by the taste, aroma, and appearance of his or her clear soup.

At the modest end of the spectrum, a bowl of soup is part of the holy trinity of Japanese cuisine. The simplest and the most quintessential Japanese meal consists of a bowl of soup and a dish of vegetables (often no more than a small plate of pickles) to accompany the main course of a bowl of rice.

Soup plays an important role in the home kitchen—it is easy to prepare, especially once you have mastered dashi broth, and is nourishing and easy to digest.

This chapter has three varieties of soup: dashi-based clear soups, wholesome miso soups, and thick soups that may feel more familiar to Western cooks but have a Japanese twist.

Shredded chicken in dashi broth

This simple soup sums up what this book is about—easy, tasty, healthy eating. The ingredients speak for themselves and there is no disguising them; so try to use the best-quality ingredients possible. Use konbu (kelp seaweed) and shiitake mushrooms to mask the smell of the chicken and to add umami (the fifth primary taste) to the soup.

1 lemon, cut into thick slices

2 free-range organic chicken legs

4³/₄ cups water

2 onions, peeled and halved

1 carrot, halved lengthwise

1 celery rib

1 garlic clove, slightly crushed
  with the flat side of a knife

1 postcard-sized piece of konbu
  (kelp seaweed)

1 dried shiitake mushroom

salt and black pepper

1 teaspoon rice vinegar

Place the lemon slices and chicken legs in a saucepan. Add enough water to cover and bring to a boil over a moderate heat. Reduce the heat to low and simmer for 10 minutes before removing the chicken. Rinse the chicken legs under cold running water and pat them dry with paper towels. Squeeze the lemon slices in your hand, letting the juice pour over the chicken.

In a large saucepan, put in the 4³/₄ cups water, chicken, onions, carrot, celery, garlic, konbu, and shiitake. Bring to a boil over a moderate heat. Reduce the heat to low and simmer for 30 minutes, skimming off any scum that floats to the surface. Remove and discard all the solid ingredients except the chicken. Let the broth simmer 10 minutes longer. Adjust the seasoning with salt and pepper before turning off the heat. Leave the chicken in the broth and let cool to room temperature.

Discard the skin from the chicken and shred the meat with a fork. If you are keeping the broth for a day or two before serving, add a pinch of salt before refrigerating.

To serve, reheat the broth, add the rice vinegar, and taste, adjusting the seasoning as needed. Arrange the shredded chicken in warmed soup bowls. Gently ladle the broth over the chicken and serve.

Kyoto bean soup

This is a Japanese interpretation of Tuscan bean soup. Like its Italian counterpart, this soup is wholesome and nourishing. The addition of miso paste gives a hidden depth without changing the character of the soup. I use canned cannellini beans for convenience, but you can substitute any beans of your choice. If you are using dried beans, soak them with three times their volume of water overnight and cook slowly until soft.

1 tablespoon vegetable oil

1 red onion, finely chopped

4–6 pieces thick-sliced unsmoked
  bacon, chopped

1 carrot, coarsely chopped
  into chunks

4 ounces burdock root, peeled
  and coarsely chopped, soaked
  in water

4 cups (1 pound) Chinese
  cabbage, coarsely chopped

4 medium rutabagas, peeled and
  cut into bite-sized chunks

4³/4 cups dashi broth
  (see pages 16–17)

4 tablespoons sake

3–4 tablespoons light soy sauce

1 cup canned cannellini beans,
  drained

2 tablespoons medium-colored
  miso paste

salt to taste

2 scallions, finely chopped

2 teaspoons toasted
  sesame seeds

Heat the vegetable oil in a large saucepan over a moderate heat and sauté the onion until softened but not browned. Add the bacon and cook for 5 minutes before adding the carrot, burdock, cabbage, and rutabagas. Sauté until soft. Pour in the dashi broth and season with sake and soy sauce. Bring to a boil, skimming off any scum that floats to the surface. Reduce the heat to low/moderate and add the beans. Let simmer for 15 minutes.

Stir in the miso paste gently and adjust the seasoning with salt. Ladle into warmed soup bowls. Garnish with the chopped scallions and sesame seeds and serve.

Cook's tip

For a vegetarian soup, omit the bacon and use vegetarian dashi broth (see page 16).
If you can't find burdock, use celery root instead.

Porgy in clear dashi broth

The Japanese love sea bream (porgy). The fish is prized not only for its fine taste and firm texture but also because it is regarded as a good omen. The traditional recipe uses an inexpensive fish head, but I think fillets are less intimidating.

4 porgy fillets, skin on,
  each weighing about 1 ounce
1½–2 teaspoons salt
4¾ cups dashi broth
  (see pages 16–17)
2 tablespoons sake
2 teaspoons grated fresh lime or
  lemon zest
watercress leaves

Place the fillets on a flat basket tray, sprinkle with salt and set aside for 30 minutes. Pour boiling water over the fillets and immediately transfer them to a bowl of ice-cold water (to remove any fishy smell). Put the fillets in a saucepan containing the dashi broth and sake and bring to a boil over a moderate heat, skimming off any scum that floats to the surface. Reduce the heat to low and simmer for 5 minutes. Adjust the seasoning with salt. Gently remove the fillets and place in warmed bowls. Strain the broth and ladle it over the fish. Garnish with the citrus zest and watercress and serve.

Cook's tip
You can use any white-fleshed fish such as cod, flounder, sole, or sea bass.
If you don't have a flat basket tray, use a sieve lined with paper towels.

Fall mushroom soup

Japan's mountainous geography and temperate climate provide ideal conditions for mushrooms, and the Japanese make great use of mysterious fungi in their cooking. I am pleased that more varieties of Japanese mushrooms are becoming increasingly available to Western cooks.

4 dried shiitake mushrooms

1/3 cup warm water

1 teaspoon vegetable oil

2 ounces shiitake mushrooms, stalks
   removed and sliced

2 ounces shimeji or oyster
   mushrooms, separated

2 tablespoons sake

2 tablespoons light soy sauce

4 3/4 cups dashi broth
   (see pages 16–17)

2 teaspoons cornstarch mixed
   with 2 tablespoons water

1 free-range egg, lightly beaten

1 teaspoon rice vinegar

salt

2 scallions, sliced diagonally

Rehydrate the dried shiitake mushrooms in the warm water for 15–20 minutes or until the mushrooms become soft. Squeeze out the excess liquid and reserve it. Remove the mushroom stems and slice the caps.

Heat the vegetable oil in a large saucepan or flameproof casserole and sauté all the mushrooms for 2–3 minutes, then add the sake and light soy sauce. When the mushrooms become soft add the reserved mushroom liquid and the dashi broth and bring to a boil. Add the cornstarch solution and stir well to thicken the soup.

Let the soup return to a boil and pour the beaten egg through a slotted spoon over the soup. Move the spoon as you pour to create a swirling effect. Turn off the heat and let the swirling egg strands rise to the top. Gently stir in the rice vinegar. Adjust the seasoning with salt. Garnish with the chopped scallions and serve.

Vine-ripened tomatoes in red miso with cilantro pesto

If there is such a thing as a designer miso soup, this is it. It is a very beautiful-looking dish with a unique and sophisticated taste. I use the most famous red miso, *haccho miso*, that comes from near Nagoya. It is made of nothing but soya beans and salt, and takes three years to mature. It is almost black in color and is dry and hard with a slightly bitter taste. If you can't get haccho miso, use as dark-colored a miso paste as possible.

I make this pesto whenever I have a large amount of cilantro on hand. It is wonderful to serve as a condiment for fish or meat or as a pasta or noodle sauce. The pesto keeps up to two weeks when refrigerated in an airtight jar.

4 medium/large vine-ripened
   tomatoes
4³/₄ cups vegetarian dashi broth
   (see page 16)
4 tablespoons red miso paste

for the cilantro pesto
a large handful of fresh
   cilantro leaves and stalks
a small handful of fresh
   mint leaves
¹/₄ cup pine nuts
1 teaspoon finely chopped
   lime zest
juice of 1 lime
1 garlic clove
¹/₂–1 teaspoon salt
5 tablespoons extra virgin
   olive oil
¹/₂ teaspoon freshly ground
   black pepper

Blanch the tomatoes in boiling water for 30 seconds; immediately plunge into ice water. Peel off the skins and set aside.

Meanwhile, combine all the ingredients for the pesto in a food processor or blender and process until smooth.

Put the tomatoes in a saucepan with the dashi broth and warm over low. With a pestle and mortar, grind the miso paste with 1 tablespoon of the dashi broth from the saucepan. Add more broth and keep grinding until the mixture becomes fluid enough to pour back into the saucepan. Stir gently and let it return to a boil; then immediately turn off the heat. Place a tomato into the center of each warmed soup bowl and ladle the soup around it. Do not cover the whole tomato with the soup. Place a small dab of the pesto on top and serve.

Cook's tip

You need very ripe tomatoes for this recipe. Let your guests enjoy breaking up their whole tomato with the back of a spoon.

Eggplant, pork, and ginger miso soup

This is a Chinese Ma Po tofu-inspired recipe, but using eggplant instead of tofu provides a little extra flavor.

1 medium eggplant
½ tablespoon vegetable oil
1 shallot, minced
4 ounces ground pork
1 ounce fresh ginger, peeled and
  finely grated
1 tablespoon soy sauce
4³/₄ cups dashi broth
  (see pages 16–17)
4–6 tablespoons medium-
  colored miso paste

Chop the eggplant into small dice and soak in water for 10 minutes to lessen the bitterness. Drain well.

Heat the vegetable oil in a saucepan or wok over moderate heat. Add the shallot and sauté until soft. Add the pork and stir-fry for 5 minutes or until the meat is no longer pink. Add the drained eggplant and ginger and stir-fry for another 6–8 minutes; season with soy sauce. Pour in the dashi broth and turn up the heat to bring to a boil. Reduce the heat to low as soon as the broth begins to boil. Put the miso paste in a ladle and gradually lower it into the soup to dilute. Bring the soup back to a boil and then immediately remove from the heat and serve in warmed soup bowls.

Cook's tip

If you like a little bit of a kick, add a spoonful of Asian chile sauce and increase the amount of grated ginger.

Spring vegetable minestrone with white miso

Millions of Japanese people begin and end their day with a bowl of miso soup. Breakfast miso soups are instantly energy-giving, while a bowl of miso soup at the dinner table brings comfort. Miso is one of the essential ingredients of Japanese cuisine and is featured in many different forms, but using it in soups is probably the easiest way.

½ tablespoon vegetable oil

1 shallot, finely chopped

1 small carrot, diced

1 medium red- or white-skinned
   potato, peeled and diced

1 stalk broccoli (preferably
   broccolini or another tender-
   stem), coarsely chopped

½ cup finely chopped napa or
   Chinese cabbage

½ cup frozen or fresh peas

1 teaspoon salt

4 ounces firm cotton tofu,
   drained (see page 110) and diced

4¾ cups vegetarian dashi broth
   (see page 16)

4 tablespoons white miso paste

1 tablespoon dark-colored
   miso paste

4 tablespoons watercress

Heat the vegetable oil in a large saucepan over low heat. Add the chopped shallot and cook until soft. Add the remaining vegetables and increase heat to medium. Season with salt and sauté until soft. Add the diced tofu, pour in the dashi broth, and bring to a boil. Reduce the heat to low and simmer for 5 minutes.

Put the miso pastes in a small sieve and partially submerge it into the soup. Press the miso pastes with the back of a spoon to dissolve into the soup. Bring the soup back to a boil and immediately turn off the heat. Ladle into warmed bowls, garnish with the watercress, and serve.

Cook's tip

There are literally hundreds of varieties of miso paste, but they can be divided into three groups according to the malt ingredients: soya beans, wheat, or rice, with the rice malt making up 80 percent of miso paste produced in Japan. Miso also comes in varying colors, ranging from pale cream to steely dark brown. Color is a good indication of taste, saltiness, and texture. Generally, the darker the color, the saltier, harder, and drier the paste. Buy the medium-colored variety if you wish to get just one type.

Tofu and pea vichyssoise with mizuna pesto

Here I have swapped tofu for potatoes—a healthy exchange. This light soup has the wonderful fresh color and taste of peas. You can serve it warm but it is also delicious chilled for hot summer days.

1 tablespoon vegetable oil

1 tablespoon butter

1 onion, finely chopped

2 cups frozen or fresh peas

2 sprigs of fresh mint

4³/4 cups vegetarian dashi broth
   (see page 16)

8 ounces soft silken tofu, drained
   (see page 110) and coarsely
   broken into pieces

salt

for the mizuna pesto

a handful of mizuna or arugula
   leaves, coarsely chopped

2 tablespoons pine nuts

grated zest and juice of ¹/2 lemon

1 garlic clove

2–3 tablespoons extra virgin
   olive oil

1 heaping teaspoon miso paste

generous amount of freshly
   ground black pepper

Heat the vegetable oil and butter in a saucepan over a moderate heat and cook the onion until soft. Add the peas, mint, and dashi broth and bring to a boil. Reduce the heat and simmer for 15 minutes.

Meanwhile, combine all the ingredients for the pesto in a food processor or blender with ¹/2 teaspoon of salt. Process until smooth. Adjust the seasoning with salt and pepper.

Add the tofu to the soup and return to a boil. Take the saucepan off the heat, remove the mint leaves and reserve 1 tablespoon of peas. Working in batches if necessary, blend the soup in a food processor until smooth; adjust the seasoning with salt. If you are serving it warm, return the soup to the saucepan to re-heat. Add the reserved peas, drizzle with pesto, and serve.

Cook's tip
This recipe works equally well with fava beans, but you must remove the skins before blending to achieve a smooth, creamy texture.

Hokkaido salmon and potato miso soup

This is a hearty, robust miso soup with plenty of substance. The island of Hokkaido was Japan's equivalent of the Wild West—in the late nineteenth century pioneering farmers and miners were encouraged to open up the country's northernmost islands, and this is the kind of soup that would have sustained them.

6 ounces salmon fillet

salt

2 small red- or white-skinned
    potatoes, peeled

1 medium carrot, cut into bite-
    sized chunks

1 cup cabbage, coarsely chopped

1 leek, trimmed and sliced
    diagonally

1 teaspoon minced garlic

4³/4 cups dashi broth
    (see pages 16–17)

2–3 heaping tablespoons
    medium-colored miso paste

2 scallions, sliced diagonally

Cut the salmon fillet into bite-sized chunks, sprinkle with salt and set aside.

Chop the potatoes into bite-sized cubes and soak in water while you prepare the other vegetables. Drain the potatoes. Put the salmon and all the vegetables in a saucepan with the dashi broth and bring to a boil over a moderate heat. Reduce the heat to low and simmer for 20 minutes, spooning off any scum that floats to the surface.

Put the miso paste in a small bowl and stir in a ladle of warm soup to dilute. Add the miso mixture to the soup and stir to blend. Adjust the seasoning with salt if necessary. Let the soup return to a boil and add the scallions. Turn off the heat and serve in warmed soup bowls.

Cook's tip

I often serve this soup garnished with a pinch of chile flakes and grated ginger—guaranteed to warm up the body and soul on a cold winter night.

Asian Gazpacho with cilantro pesto

Gazpacho is the chilled raw vegetable soup from Spain. This is an equally refreshing and healthy East-meets-West version. Both tomatoes and cucumbers are known to aid digestion and have a cooling effect. This is also a tasty way to encourage fussy eaters to eat raw vegetables.

1 cucumber, peeled, seeded
  and coarsely chopped
5 very ripe medium tomatoes,
  seeded and coarsely chopped
1 small red onion, peeled and
  coarsely chopped
1 large red chile (preferably
  serrano or jalapeño), seeded
  and coarsely chopped
1–2 garlic cloves, peeled
1 tablespoon grated fresh ginger
5 tablespoons rice vinegar
juice of 2 limes
2 tablespoons soy sauce
2 tablespoons extra virgin
  olive oil
salt and black pepper to taste
a handful of fresh cilantro and
  mint leaves, finely chopped

for the cilantro pesto
1 bunch fresh cilantro, with
  stems and roots attached,
  if possible
1/2 cup pine nuts
grated zest and juice of 1 lime
1/3 cup grated Parmesan cheese
5 tablespooons extra virgin
  olive oil
salt

Put the cucumber, tomatoes, red onion, chile, and garlic in a food processor or a blender and purée. Add the ginger, rice vinegar, lime juice, soy sauce, and olive oil and purée again. Mix in the chopped cilantro and mint leaves. Adjust the seasoning with salt and black pepper and refrigerate preferably overnight (or at least 4 hours) to develop flavors.

For the pesto, blend all the ingredients with 1/2 teaspoon of salt until a coarse paste forms. Serve the soup in chilled bowls, with drizzles of pesto and olive oil over the top.

Cook's tip
It is hard to gauge the number of chiles as everyone has a different heat tolerance. My advice is to start with less than you think you would like—remember that you can always add more but can't take it out. I also recommend using larger chiles than the small bird's-eye type, which are terribly hot and make the heat level difficult to control.

Roast pumpkin soup with lime and cilantro pesto

The sweetness of autumn-ripe pumpkin is accentuated by roasting. There is an old saying in Japanese that you won't get cold if you eat pumpkins on the winter solstice. As you can imagine, I used to snicker at such sayings when I was young—but now I look at them differently. Some of these ancient practices have a curious scientific truth in them. Pumpkins are rich in vitamins A, C, and E.

2 pounds ripe pumpkin, peeled,
  seeded and cut into wedges
4 ounces elephant garlic, peeled,
  or 1 leek, trimmed
2 tablespoons olive oil
salt and black pepper
1 tablespoon granulated sugar
2 tablespoons butter
1 medium onion, finely chopped
4³/4 cups vegetarian dashi broth
  (see page 16)

**for the lime and
cilantro pesto**
grated zest and juice of 2 limes
4 cups (lightly packed) fresh
  cilantro leaves
1 garlic clove, peeled
salt and pepper

Preheat the oven to 375°F. Brush the pumpkin and garlic with the olive oil and sprinkle with 1 teaspoon of salt and the sugar. Roast in a baking sheet for 30 minutes or until soft.

Meanwhile, put all the ingredients for the pesto in a food processor or a blender with ¹/2 teaspoon each of salt and black pepper. Process until smooth.

Melt the butter in a large saucepan or flameproof casserole over a low/moderate heat and cook the chopped onion until soft.

Working in small batches, purée the roasted pumpkin, garlic, and onion with the dashi broth. Adjust the seasoning with salt and black pepper. Pour the soup into a saucepan to heat but do not let it boil. Serve in warmed bowls with dollops of pesto in the center.

Cook's tip
This is a warming and comforting soup—serve with crusty whole wheat bread.

vegetables

Vegetables play an important role in Japanese cooking. They are part of the holy trinity of the most quintessential form of a Japanese meal—*ichi ju issai* (it literally means one soup and one vegetable) to accompany a bowl of rice. We eat more vegetables than in the West, where the tradition of "meat and two veggies" still seems to live on. In the post-economic depression era of the early twenty-first century, Japanese consumers have become discerning, demanding more and better-quality seasonal vegetables.

There are many ways of cooking vegetables in Japanese cuisine—raw, pickled, vinegar-flavored; or dressed with other ingredients such as tofu, sesame seeds, and miso paste; boiled, steamed, stir-fried, simmered, grilled, or deep-fried. Vegetables are treated with the same respect as fish and meat in preparing a balanced meal, with taste, color, nutrition, and texture taken into consideration.

One striking feature of Japanese cooking with any ingredient, but especially with vegetables, is the emphasis placed on seasonality. Non-Japanese people may find it almost impossible to understand the passion that a little vegetable can arouse and the trouble some Japanese cooks are prepared to endure in order to secure the season's best offerings, but their efforts will be appreciated at the table. Eating what is in season is the best way for both taste and nutrition and almost always the most economical. I urge you to get to know which seasons are best for which vegetables in your own area and try supporting local growers and farmers' markets as much as possible.

These recipes are not necessarily vegetarian, but give vegetables the same respect as fish or meat. Many of these recipes can be eaten as appetizers or main courses, not just as side dishes.

Stir-fry of snow peas and scallops with ginger

I love the Japanese name for snow peas, *kinusaya*, which means silk pod (they are as soft and rubbing them together makes the sound of rustling silk). They are very rich in vitamin C because they are picked while they are still growing. The quick stir-frying method and the addition of scallops make this recipe a great dish for keeping the skin beautiful and helping you to recover from fatigue.

8 ounces snow peas

8 ounces sea scallops

3 tablespoons sake

1 tablespoon cornstarch

salt and black pepper

1 tablespoon vegetable oil

1 (1-inch) piece of fresh ginger,
   peeled and thinly sliced

5 tablespoons dashi broth
   (see pages 16–17)

1 teaspoon rice vinegar

1 teaspoon Asian sesame oil

Remove the strings from the snow peas. Cut the scallops in half horizontally and place in a bowl. Add 1 tablespoon of the sake, the cornstarch, and a pinch of salt. Toss to coat.

Heat a wok or large skillet, add the vegetable oil, and sauté the ginger slices to flavor the oil. Add the scallops and stir-fry for 3 minutes. Add the snow peas and cook 3 minutes longer. Add the dashi stock and bring to a boil, then add the remaining sake, the vinegar, and sesame oil and return to a boil before turning off the heat. Adjust the seasoning with salt and pepper and serve.

Purple sprouting broccoli with mustard soy dressing

Sprouting broccoli is almost identical to an old Japanese brassica called nanohana in its appearance, taste, and nutritional value. They are both great health-giving vegetables with high carotene, vitamins B2 and C, and are rich in minerals. They help to develop the body's natural resistance to ward off colds, lower blood pressure, prevent arteriosclerosis, improve the condition of the skin, and prevent anemia. Purple sprouting broccoli is at its best in late winter and very early spring. Do not overcook it as that will destroy its valuable vitamin C content.

1 pound purple sprouting broccoli
(see Cook's tip)

for the mustard soy dressing
3/4 cup vegetarian dashi broth
(see page 16)
2 teaspoons light soy sauce
2 teaspoons mirin
2 tablespoons English mustard
powder mixed with
1/4 cup water

Trim the broccoli stalks. Bring a large saucepan of salted water to a boil and cook a quarter of the broccoli for 1–2 minutes or until the color has deepened. Transfer the cooked broccoli on to a flat basket to drain and fan to cool it down. Repeat the process three more times to cook the rest of the broccoli. (Working in small batches shortens the cooking time and helps to preserve the deep green and purple color of the vegetable.)

When cool enough to handle, gently squeeze the broccoli to rid it of excess water and lay it on a flat dish. Mix together all the ingredients for the mustard soy dressing and pour over the broccoli. Let sit 20 minutes to let the flavors develop, and then serve at room temperature.

Cook's tip
When purple sprouting broccoli is not available, substitute another tender-stemmed broccoli such as broccolini or broccoli rabe.

Japanese spring cabbage coleslaw

There is no doubt that cabbage suffers from bad publicity—the mere mention of the vegetable often provokes dispiriting memories of dull institutional meals. I think this is quite unfair for one of the most accessible and healthy vegetables around. Cabbages have a unique nutrient called vitamin U that is beneficial to the digestive system and prevents fat building on the liver. They are also rich in vitamin C—two or three leaves provide half your daily vitamin C requirement. Here is a delicious, quick and easy recipe to encourage you and your family to eat more cabbage.

8 ounces napa or Chinese cabbage

½ medium carrot, peeled and cut into matchstick-sized pieces

8 ounces deep-fried tofu

**for the mustard
miso dressing**

1 teaspoon English mustard powder, mixed with 1 tablespoon water

1 teaspoon sugar

2 teaspoons light-colored miso paste

1 tablespoon soy sauce

3 tablespoons vegetarian dashi broth (see page 16) or water

Cut away and discard the core and thick ribs of the cabbage; slice the leaves into fine shreds. Blanch the cabbage and carrot in boiling water for 2–3 minutes and then immediately transfer to a bowl of ice water; remove and squeeze them gently to drain off as much water as possible. Meanwhile, heat a skillet and sauté the deep-fried tofu on both sides. When cool enough to handle, slice into thin strips. Mix together all the ingredients for the mustard miso dressing. Put the drained cabbage, carrot, and tofu strips in a bowl and add the dressing. Toss gently to coat the mixture and serve.

Grilled asparagus in dashi

Asparagus was introduced to Japan by the Dutch in the late eighteenth century and was originally grown as an ornamental plant. It is a wonderful vegetable that comes into season in late spring. It's asparagine converts to amino acid when digested, which aids a healthy metabolism, energizes the body and promotes healthy skin. Green asparagus is more nutritious than the white variety.

20 asparagus spears (about
  1 pound)
2 tablespoons vegetable oil
1/3 cup dashi broth
  (see pages 16–17)
3 tablespoons soy sauce
1 1/2 tablespoons mirin

Bend the asparagus spears at their natural breaking point and discard the woody lower parts. Brush each spear with vegetable oil and grill (or use a ridged broiler pan) for 5–10 minutes (depending on thickness), turning them to cook evenly. Meanwhile, combine the dashi broth, soy sauce and mirin in a flat dish. Transfer the cooked asparagus spears to the dish while they are hot to let them absorb the flavor of the dashi mixture. Serve warm or at room temperature.

Gently simmered bamboo shoots with chicken

My grandfather and I used to go into dew-covered bamboo groves on early spring mornings to dig up young bamboo shoots. I remember having to tread carefully to avoid the tiny shoots whose tips were just pushing through the surface. We used to rush back with a big basketful of them for my grandmother to cook right away.

4 ounces boneless
   chicken, minced
1 (1-inch) piece fresh ginger,
   peeled and finely shredded
1 can (about 14 ounces) bamboo
   shoots, drained and cut into
   large chunks
2¹/₂ cups dashi broth
   (see pages 16–17)
3 tablespoons sake
3 tablespoons mirin
pinch of salt
2¹/₂ tablespoons light soy sauce

Heat a saucepan and cook the chicken, stirring constantly to prevent sticking.

Divide the ginger shreds into two equal portions and soak one portion in cold water. Add the other half of the ginger, the bamboo shoots, and the dashi broth to the chicken and bring to a boil. Reduce the heat and add the sake, mirin, salt, and soy sauce. Simmer for 10 minutes. Turn off the heat and let cool. Drain the reserved ginger and sprinkle over each serving. If you prefer to serve this dish warm, gently reheat it.

Simmered fava beans with bacon

Like other varieties of beans, fava beans are packed with protein, calcium, and other minerals and are rich in B vitamins that work to reduce fatigue and prevent hardening of the arteries.

3 pounds fava beans, shelled
2 tablespoons vegetable oil
¹/₂ cup bacon bits
1 teaspoon Asian sesame oil

for the cooking liquid
2 tablespoons sake
1 teaspoon grated fresh ginger
¹/₃ cup dashi broth (see pages 16–17)
1 tablespoon soy sauce
2 teaspoons sugar

Blanch the shelled fava beans for 3 minutes and drain. Heat a wok or skillet over a moderate heat, add the vegetable oil and sauté the bacon bits. Add the sake, ginger, broth, soy sauce, and sugar and cook for 3 minutes, skimming off any scum that floats to the surface.

Increase the heat to high and add the fava beans; cook 3 minutes. Adjust the seasoning with salt if needed. Add the sesame oil just before you turn off the heat and then serve.

Avocado dip with wasabi miso

The Guinness Book of Records lists the avocado as the most nutritious fruit in the world. Although it has double the calories of milk and four times as much fat, it is non-saturated fat, which helps to lower cholesterol. The avocado also contains nine varieties of vitamins including B, C, and vitamin E, that work together to slow down the aging process. It is rich in minerals, especially kalium, that lowers blood pressure, and is high in edible fiber. Although the avocado is a recent addition to the Japanese table, it marries well with many Japanese ingredients.

2 very ripe avocados

2 teaspoons wasabi powder,
   mixed with 4 teaspoons water

1 teaspoon soy sauce

½ tablespoon medium-colored
   miso paste

1 teaspoon rice vinegar

Halve the avocados lengthwise; twist to separate the halves and discard the pits. Discard the peel and mash the flesh in a bowl with a fork. Add the wasabi powder mixture, soy sauce, miso paste, and rice vinegar, and continue to mash until it is well blended into a smooth mixture. Serve with raw vegetables or breadsticks.

Cook's tip

The addition of the rice vinegar helps to maintain the avocado's bright green color as well as taking a slight edge off the richness. Keep the dip covered with plastic wrap until needed.

Tomato and tofu salad with tomato dressing

A bright red tomato is a symbol of hot summer days. Not only is it beautiful but a highly health-giving vegetable that lowers blood pressure, too. It helps you recover from fatigue and maintain a good digestive system but, most of all, it is known to have anti-carcinogenic properties.

4 large vine-ripened tomatoes

8 ounces soft silken tofu, drained
   (see page 110)

freshly ground black pepper

12 fresh basil leaves, torn

for the tomato dressing

2 large vine-ripened tomatoes

1 teaspoon light soy sauce

1 tablespoon extra virgin olive oil

For the tomato dressing, blanch the tomatoes in boiling water for 30 seconds; then immediately plunge into ice water. Remove and discard the skins and seeds and put the tomatoes in a food processor with the soy sauce and olive oil. Process for a few seconds or until smooth.

Meanwhile, cut the other tomatoes and tofu into thick slices and divide into four equal portions. Arrange the tomato and tofu slices on individual plates. Pour the tomato dressing on top and sprinkle with freshly ground black pepper. Garnish with the basil and serve.

Cucumber and steamed chicken salad with sesame ginger dressing

Over ninety percent of a cucumber is water, and its hydrating, diuretic, and cooling effects have long been recognized in Chinese medicine. To take full advantage of its refreshing taste and texture, it is best to keep cooking to a minimum.

1 boneless, skinless chicken breast
  half (about 6 ounces)
pinch of salt
1 tablespoon sake
2 small cucumbers
1/2 teaspoon Asian sesame oil
2 scallions, finely chopped

for the sesame ginger dressing
4 tablespoons toasted
  sesame seeds
1 1/2 tablespoons sugar
1 1/2 tablespoons rice vinegar
2 tablespoons soy sauce
1 teaspoon peeled, grated
  fresh ginger
1 teaspoon medium-colored
  miso paste

Put the chicken breast on a small dish, rub it with salt and drizzle with sake. Place it in a steamer basket over simmering water. Cook, covered, for 10–15 minutes, until chicken is white throughout. Set aside to cool.

Meanwhile, cut the cucumbers into wedge-shaped chunks.

For the dressing, use a pestle and mortar to grind the sesame seeds into a coarse paste. Add the sugar, rice vinegar, soy sauce, ginger, and miso and continue to grind into a smooth paste.

Shred the chicken breast with a fork. Put the shredded chicken and cucumber chunks in a large mixing bowl, drizzle with the sesame oil and miso dressing and toss well to coat. Transfer to a serving dish, garnish with the chopped scallions, and serve.

Stir-fry of red and yellow bell peppers with beef

This is my adaptation of a traditional Chinese recipe to suit my children who were less than enthusiastic about the green peppers and bamboo shoots, but did enjoy red and yellow peppers. Nutritionally, all peppers are rich in a vitamin C that does not break down in the cooking process. Both the red and yellow varieties have twice as much vitamin C as the green variety combined with a lemon. Vitamin C is good for the skin and helps the body to recover from fatigue.

1 red bell pepper

1 yellow bell pepper

8 ounces beef fillet

2 tablespoons vegetable oil

1 teaspoon sugar

3 tablespoons soy sauce

2 tablespoons sake

2 teaspoons oyster sauce

freshly ground black pepper

for the beef marinade

1/3 teaspoon salt

1 tablespoon sake

1 free-range egg, beaten

3 tablespoons cornstarch

Cut the peppers into quarters and remove the seeds and white membrane inside. Slice into thin strips. Cut the beef into thin strips. Mix all the ingredients for the marinade in a bowl and stir in the beef. Let sit 10 minutes to absorb the flavor.

Heat a wok or skillet and add the vegetable oil. Stir-fry the peppers for 3 minutes, then add the beef and cook 5 minutes. Lower the heat, sprinkle the sugar and drizzle the soy sauce and sake around the edge of the wok. Add the sugar and oyster sauce, season with black pepper, and mix well. Turn off the heat and serve.

元
気

Japanese new potato salad with tofu mayonnaise

There is nothing quite like digging up home-grown potatoes from the warm ground on an early summer's day. At this time, before the sun bakes the earth, you can pull out a plant by hand and a dozen or so golf-ball-sized pale new potatoes tumble out. Although the main nutrient in potatoes is carbohydrate, they are rich in vitamins B1 and C (that doesn't break down during cooking) and potassium, which lowers blood pressure. They also contain plenty of edible fiber. Here is a quick and easy way to enjoy the full taste and nutrients of new potatoes.

8 ounces new potatoes, washed
and scrubbed

for the tofu mayonnaise
12 ounces tofu (silken soft
or firm)
1/2 tablespoon sesame seeds,
ground to a smooth paste
1 1/2 tablespoons light-colored
miso paste
1 1/2 tablespoons sugar
1 teaspoon light soy sauce
1 teaspoon mirin
1 tablespoon rice vinegar
pinch of salt

Drain the tofu (see page 110). You can use either silken soft or firm cotton tofu, but soft tofu has a higher water content and therefore needs more time to drain. The drained tofu should be half of its original size and feel solid.

Put the tofu, sesame seed paste, miso paste, sugar, soy sauce, and mirin in a food processor or blender and process until very smooth. Add the vinegar to blend and adjust the taste with salt if needed. Ideally the tofu mayonnaise should be eaten the same day it is made, but can be kept up to 3 days in the refrigerator.

Boil the potatoes in a large saucepan of water until tender. Let the potatoes cool before tossing them with 2–3 tablespoons of the tofu mayonnaise, and then serve.

Cook's tip
It is best not to use too much tofu mayonnaise so that the taste of the potatoes is not overshadowed. The creamy mild mayonnaise goes well with practically any cooked vegetable. Also try using it as a dip with a difference.

String beans with sesame miso dressing

String beans are also known as Kenyan or French beans or simply green beans. In the western part of Japan, the beans are sometimes called *sandomame*, which means three times beans because their fast growth allows them to be harvested three times in a year. String beans contain well-balanced B vitamins that help you to recover from fatigue, prevent fat accumulating in the liver and stops the hardening of arteries. Rolling the beans with a small amount of salt on a chopping board keeps the bright green color after boiling.

8 ounces fresh string beans

1 tablespoon salt

1 teaspoon toasted sesame seeds

**for the sesame
miso dressing**

2 tablespoons toasted
 sesame seeds

1 teaspoon sugar

1 teaspoon light/medium-
 colored miso paste

1 tablespoon soy sauce

Trim the string beans and spread them on a chopping board. Sprinkle with the salt and, using the palms of your hands, gently roll the beans back and forth a few times. Bring a large saucepan of water to a boil and cook the beans for 3 minutes, and then drain well.

Meanwhile, for the dressing, put the sesame seeds in a mortar and grind them to a coarse paste. Add the sugar, miso paste, and soy sauce and continue to grind until the mixture becomes smooth and uniform. Transfer the beans to a bowl, add the dressing and mix well to coat the beans. Sprinkle with sesame seeds to garnish and serve.

Grilled corn with teriyaki sauce

Maize is one of the three major grains grown in the world. It is rich in vitamin B and E, that work to prevent oxidization of cells and thereby slows down the aging process. It is also rich in edible fiber, which prevents constipation and colon cancer.

4 medium ears of corn on the cob

2 tablespoons vegetable oil

4 tablespoons teriyaki sauce
  (see page 167)

Cut the corn cobs crosswise into 1¹/₂ inch pieces. Cook in boiling water for 2–3 minutes, then drain. Brush with the oil and place under a preheated broiler or on a grill to cook, turning, for 5 minutes or until parts become golden brown and begin to caramelize. Remove from the heat, brush with the teriyaki sauce, and serve.

Zucchini and tuna chunks with garlic

Every year, I grow a few zucchini plants for their flowers and fruit. They are prolific, large, sprawling plants. I have many zucchini recipes that use both the flowers and the vegetables. This recipe is one of my family's favorite items on our summer table. Nutritionally, zucchini are a cross between cucumbers and pumpkins—they are rich in carotene, which strengthens the mucous membranes and aids the body's natural resistance.

pinch of salt

6 to 8 ounces fresh tuna steak

1 tablespoon vegetable oil

2 garlic cloves, thinly sliced

2–3 medium zucchini, cut into thick slices

3 tablespoons soy sauce

1½ tablespoons rice vinegar

freshly ground black pepper

Sprinkle salt over the tuna steak and set aside.

Heat a skillet and add the vegetable oil, reduce the heat to low and cook the sliced garlic until it turns golden and crisp. Remove the garlic slices with a slotted spoon and set aside.

Increase the heat to high and cook the tuna steak for 1 minute on each side. Remove the steak to a chopping board and let cool before cutting into bite-sized cubes.

Replenish the oil in the pan if necessary and reduce the heat to moderate. Cook the zucchini slices until they turn golden brown on both sides. Add the tuna cubes and season with the soy sauce and vinegar. Transfer the mixture to a serving plate, sprinkle with the garlic slices, season with black pepper and serve.

Cook's tip

I often serve this with pasta as a one-course lunch.

Spicy edamame

Edamame used to be young soya beans harvested early, until the end of the seventeenth century when special edamame breeds were developed. Like their older brother, edamame are rich in protein, minerals, calcium, and vitamin B1 but also in vitamin C, which is absent in soya beans. Edamame also contain a type of amino acid that protects the kidneys and liver from the harmful effects of alcohol. In Japan, edamame are one of the favorite accompaniments served with beer. They are in season in the summer when they are sold fresh in their pods, but they are also available frozen throughout the year.

*1 pound fresh or frozen
    edamame (in pods)*
2 fresh red chiles
2 tablespoons soy sauce
2 teaspoons rice vinegar

Put the edamame and the chiles in a large saucepan of water and bring to a boil. Cook for 3 minutes, scooping out any scum that floats to the surface. Be careful not to overcook the beans. Drain and reserve the chiles. Pour the soy sauce and vinegar over the beans while they are still hot and toss to coat. Serve either at room temperature or chilled, garnished with the chiles, if you like.

Stir-fried carrots and deep-fried tofu

Carrots have long been regarded as a warming vegetable beneficial to the lungs and spleen, which control blood quality. As well as having anti-carcinogenic properties, their high carotene level converts into vitamin A when digested and helps the body's natural immune system.

4 medium carrots

2 sheets deep-fried tofu

2 tablespoons vegetable oil

3 tablespoons dashi broth
  (see pages 16–17)

2 tablespoons light soy sauce

2 tablespoons sugar

1 teaspoon Asian sesame oil

2 tablespoons toasted sesame seeds

Cut the carrots into matchstick-sized pieces. Place the deep-fried tofu in a sieve and pour over boiling water to remove any excess oil. Cut it into thin strips. Heat a wok or skillet and add the vegetable oil. Stir-fry the carrots for 3 minutes, then add the dashi broth, soy sauce, and sugar. Reduce the heat to low and continue to cook until the liquid has evaporated. Add the sesame oil and stir well before turning off the heat. Sprinkle with sesame seeds and serve.

Steamed eggplant with spicy miso dressing

There is an old saying in Japanese that you should not let your daughter-in-law eat an eggplant in autumn. One unkind interpretation is that this is because eggplants are at their best in autumn and a wicked mother-in-law thinks they are too good for her daughter-in-law. But a kinder interpretation is that eggplants have a cooling effect and lower your body temperature.

2 medium eggplants

1 garlic clove, peeled and grated

1 (1-inch) piece of fresh ginger,
  peeled and grated

1 shallot, minced

3 tablespoons soy sauce

1 tablespoon medium-colored
  miso paste

2 tablespoons rice vinegar

1 tablespoon toasted sesame seeds

1 teaspoon Asian sesame oil

Cut off and discard the eggplant stems and quarter them lengthwise. Soak them in water for 10 minutes to reduce the bitterness. Drain and pat dry with paper towels. Steam the eggplants for 12-15 minutes or until they are soft in the middle. Lay them out flat on a chopping board and fan them to cool down.

Mix together all the other ingredients for the dressing. Transfer the eggplant to a serving dish, drizzle with the dressing and serve.

Cook's tip

Do not refrigerate eggplant, as they prefer warmer temperatures and refrigeration toughens the skin. Try to use eggplant within a day or two after purchase.

Daikon salad with watercress and walnuts

The giant white radish is called daikon in Japanese, which means a big root. Although it is not native to the country, it is the most widely cultivated vegetable in Japan and used extensively in its cuisine. Known as a natural digestive, it is nearly always served with grilled fish. It is rich in vitamins A, C, and E, but the health benefits of its vitamin C content can be lost by peeling, cooking, and grating too far in advance of serving. It is also a marvelous natural remedy for a hangover—a cupful of grated daikon should do the trick.

*8 ounces daikon (Japanese
  white radish)*
pinch of salt
1 tablespoon rice vinegar
*1 small bunch watercress, tough
  stems removed*
*6 walnuts, shelled and
  coarsely chopped*

for the dressing
2 tablespoons rice vinegar
*2 tablespoons extra virgin
  olive oil*
2 teaspoons minced shallot
2 teaspoons light soy sauce
1 teaspoon sugar
freshly ground black pepper

Cut the daikon into thin slices, and then cut the slices into matchstick-sized pieces. Put them in a bowl, sprinkle with the salt and vinegar, and set aside for 10 minutes.

Meanwhile, mix all the ingredients for the dressing. Lightly squeeze the daikon to remove any excess liquid, and place it in a salad bowl with the watercress and walnut pieces. Drizzle with the dressing, toss gently to mix, and serve.

Shimeji mushrooms and ginkgo nut parcel

In Japanese cooking, mushrooms are culinary seasonal symbols for autumn. They contain vitamin B2, which lowers cholesterol, and vitamin D that helps the body to absorb calcium. They are rich in edible fiber and have no calories, which makes them an ideal diet food. Shimeji mushrooms are renowned for their flavor: they contain high levels of an amino acid that gives umami (the fifth element of taste).

2 packets shimeji mushrooms

¼ cup extra virgin olive oil

2 garlic cloves, peeled and
   crushed with the side of a knife

12 ginkgo nuts* (sold ready to
   use in vacuum packs or cans in
   Asian markets)

½ teaspoon salt

4 thick slices of lime

4 (12-inch) squares of
   aluminum foil

*if using the canned variety,
   rinse off the brine

Preheat the oven to 350°F. Cut off the base off of the mushrooms and separate them (or if desired, keep them in little clumps). Heat a skillet over a moderate heat and add the garlic to the olive oil to flavor. Remove the garlic when it turns golden. Increase the heat and quickly sauté the mushrooms and gingko nuts; season with the salt.

Divide the mushrooms into four equal portions and transfer each portion into the center of an aluminum foil sheet. Add a lime slice to each one and gather up the corners to make parcels. Make the parcels as roomy as possible so as not to crowd the ingredients. Put them on a baking sheet and bake them for 5 minutes. Serve unopened and let your guests enjoy the fragrance as they open them at the table.

Roasted sweet potatoes with soy honey glaze

Sweet potatoes saved the Japanese from a nationwide famine in 1732, and food shortages during the World Wars and immediate post-war periods. The main nutritional component of sweet potatoes is carbohydrate, twice as high as that of ordinary potatoes. They are a high-energy-giving vegetable. They also have stable vitamin C, equivalent to that of grapefruit, which can withstand cooking heat. The sweet potato's edible fiber promotes a healthy colon, prevents constipation, and carries cholesterol out of the body to protect it against colon cancer and hardening of the arteries. Stone-baked sweet potatoes wrapped in newspaper from street vendors were a popular snack when I was growing up in Japan. It was truly a comfort food. I hope to bring back that sweet memory of my childhood with this recipe. The sweetness increases with the slow roasting.

1 pound sweet potatoes, peeled

3 tablespoons vegetable oil

1 teaspoon Asian sesame oil

pinch of salt

for the soy honey glaze

2 tablespoons honey

1 tablespoon soy sauce

1 teaspoon juice from grated
  fresh ginger

1 tablespoon toasted
  sesame seeds

Preheat the oven to 350°F. Cut the sweet potatoes into ice-cube-sized dice. Put the potatoes in a single layer on a baking sheet and drizzle with the vegetable and sesame oils. With clean hands, mix the potatoes to coat them with the oils and sprinkle with salt. Place the sheet on the middle shelf of the oven and roast for 30–40 minutes or until the edges turn crisp.

Preheat the broiler to its highest setting. Mix the honey, soy sauce, and ginger juice for the glaze. Drizzle over the potatoes and place 4 to 6 inches from the broiler. Broil 5–7 minutes, shaking the baking sheet occasionally, until nicely browned on the outside and tender inside. Sprinkle with the sesame seeds and serve.

Cook's tip

To extract the juice from grated ginger, simply squeeze it and discard the fibrous remains left in your fingers.

Cauliflower miso gratin

This is a Japanese version of cauliflower au gratin—a soul-warming, comforting dish. Raw cauliflower has less vitamin C than its green brother, broccoli, but they are almost equal when cooked. In other words, cauliflower's vitamin C is heat-resistant and does not break down during cooking, making this an ideal vegetable for the winter.

8 ounces cauliflower florets,
   cut into small chunks
1 medium carrot, cut into
   small chunks
4 to 6 ounces broccoli spears, cut
   into small chunks
8 ounces soft silken tofu, left
   wrapped in paper towels
   to drain
2 tablespoons butter
1 tablespoon all-purpose flour
1/3 cup 2% reduced fat milk
1/3 cup vegetarian dashi broth
   (see page 16)
2 tablespoons miso paste
salt and black pepper
2 tablespoons grated
   Parmesan cheese

Preheat the oven to 400°F. Blanch the cauliflower, carrot, and broccoli in boiling water and set aside to drain. Cut the tofu into bite-sized cubes. Melt the butter in a saucepan and whisk in the flour to blend. Whisk in the milk and dashi until smooth. Dilute the miso paste with a little of the mixture and then add it to the pan, stir well and turn off the heat. Adjust the seasoning with salt and pepper. Put the vegetables and tofu in a buttered ovenproof gratin dish and pour the sauce over the top. Sprinkle with grated Parmesan and bake for 15–20 minutes or until bubbly-hot.

Cook's tip
Adding vinegar to boiling water keeps the cauliflower white. You can use any miso of your choice, but the lighter color is less salty and better suited for this recipe.

Warm bean sprout salad with crispy garlic

There is no season for bean sprouts—they are available throughout the year. They have all the health benefits of ordinary beans—proteins, B vitamins, calcium, iron, and plenty of edible fiber. But vitamin C, which is absent in ordinary beans, is found in bean sprouts.

8 ounces bean sprouts, roots
  removed
3 tablespoons vegetable oil
1 teaspoon sesame oil
2 garlic cloves, thinly sliced
1/2 teaspoon crushed hot red
  pepper flakes
1 tablespoon soy sauce
pinch of salt
1 tablespoon toasted
  sesame seeds

Blanch the bean sprouts in boiling water and drain well. Heat a skillet over a moderate heat and add both the vegetable and sesame oils. Add the garlic slices and cook, stirring, until crisp and golden. Remove the garlic slices to a piece of paper towel to drain. Increase the heat to high, add the bean sprouts and toss well to coat each sprout with the oil. Keep this very brief—it is only to heat the sprouts, not to cook them. Add the pepper flakes and soy sauce, adjust the seasoning with salt and turn off the heat. Transfer to a warm serving dish, sprinkle with the garlic slices and sesame seeds and serve.

Roast pumpkin and garlic mash

One of my grandmother's pet subjects was how to avoid getting a cold, and she had a theory that involved eating pumpkin on the winter solstice. It contains plenty of carotene, which converts to vitamin A when it is digested and strengthens the body's immunity. It is also rich in vitamins C and E, which prevent hardening of the arteries and slow aging. On top of all these benefits, it is a truly comforting vegetable with its bright color, smooth texture, and sweet nutty taste.

1 sugar pumpkin or other small
  pumpkin, seeded and cut into
  4 equal-sized pieces
4 garlic cloves, peeled
2 tablespoons vegetable oil
salt
1/2 teaspoon Asian sesame oil
2 tablespoons mirin
1 teaspoon medium-colored
  miso paste

Preheat the oven to 400°F. Put the pumpkin pieces, skin-side down, on a baking sheet with the garlic cloves. Brush with vegetable oil and sprinkle with a pinch of salt. Roast for 45 minutes or until very soft and the edges have become caramelized. When it is cool enough to handle, scoop out the flesh from the skin. Put the pumpkin flesh and garlic in a food processor or blender, add the sesame oil, mirin, and miso and process until very smooth. Adjust the seasoning with salt and serve.

Spicy stir-fried spinach with pancetta

I love spinach—it is easy to grow, easy to cook, has a beautiful, deep green color and, above all, is very tasty and packed with natural goodness. Spinach has long been recognized as a power-giving vegetable with a high iron content. It is also rich in carotene, which converts into vitamin A, B vitamins, and vitamin C. Of all the vegetables, spinach contains the second most betacarotene, after carrots, that is known to have anti-carcinogenic properties. This is absorbed more efficiently if eaten with oil and fat. Spinach's natural season is late autumn and winter when one needs all the natural remedies to stay healthy.

1 pound spinach leaves,
  well-rinsed
2 tablespoons vegetable oil
4 ounces pancetta or bacon bits
2 tablespoons medium-colored
  miso paste
2 tablespoons sake
1 teaspoon crushed hot red
  pepper flakes

Chop the spinach into ½-inch pieces. Heat a wok or large skillet over a moderate heat and add the vegetable oil. Fry the pancetta or bacon bits until crisp. Add the miso paste and cook for 1 minute, then add the spinach and sprinkle with sake. Quickly toss the spinach to coat with the cooking juices. Turn off the heat—do not overcook the spinach as the residual heat is sufficient to wilt the leaves. Sprinkle with the pepper flakes and serve.

Pot au feu of Chinese cabbage and bacon

Chinese cabbage is one of the most popular vegetables used in Japanese cooking. Although it is now available throughout the year, its natural season is winter. It is a valuable source of vitamin C and minerals such as iron, magnesium, and potassium. It is used in many hotpots as slow cooking makes it sweet and easy to digest. This recipe is designed to provide a hearty big soup to warm the body and soul.

1 pound thick-sliced unsmoked
   bacon such as pancetta,
   preferably with the
   rind removed
1 (1½-inch piece) fresh ginger,
   peeled and grated
2 pounds Chinese or napa
   cabbage, quartered lengthwise
¾ cup sake
2½ cups water
4 tablespoons light soy sauce
1 tablespoon rice vinegar
¼ cup scallions, finely chopped

for the lime condiment
2 limes
1 garlic clove, peeled
½ teaspoon salt

Divide the bacon and grated ginger into four equal portions and subdivide each portion into thirds. Insert bacon slices and a dab of grated ginger between the leaves of each cabbage quarter. Continue to make bacon layers until you have used up one portion. Tie the cabbage quarter with a piece of cooking string to hold it together. Repeat the process to make three more servings. Place the four cabbage quarters in a large saucepan and add the sake and water. Put the lid on and bring to a boil over a moderate heat. Reduce the heat and simmer for 30 minutes.

Meanwhile, for the lime condiment, remove the zest and chop it finely. Halve the limes and extract the juice. Put the lime juice, zest, garlic, and salt in a mortar and pound until a smooth paste forms.

Add the soy sauce and rice vinegar to the cabbage soup and keep warm. Remove the cabbage quarters and let them cool before cutting into large bite-sized pieces. Reheat the soup if necessary. Place the cabbage in individual serving bowls, ladle the soup over the top, garnish with the chopped scallions, and pass the lime condiment at the table.

Cook's tip
I suggest you serve this with crusty whole wheat bread.

Leek and carrot mini "frittatas"

A Japanese chef friend of mine got very exited when he spotted leeks on sale. He mistook them for a variety of Japanese long white scallions. The two are not the same but make very good alternatives to each other. Leeks have nutritional values similar to onions and garlic—they are warming, improve blood circulation, and prevent fatigue and backache.

2 medium leeks

1 medium carrot, cut into
   matchstick-sized pieces

2 free-range eggs, lightly beaten

1/4 cup water

1/4 cup all-purpose flour

2 tablespoons cornstarch

1/2 teaspoon salt

2 tablespoons vegetable oil

for the dipping sauce

1/4 cup soy sauce

1 teaspoon Asian sesame oil

2 tablespoons rice vinegar

Trim the leeks, halve lengthwise, and slice thinly. Put the leeks and carrot in a mixing bowl, add the eggs, water, flour, cornstarch, and salt and mix well.

Heat a large nonstick skillet and add the vegetable oil. Divide the leek mixture into eight equal portions and, with a tablespoon, drop each portion into the heated pan. Cook for 3 minutes, then turn each small disc to cook the other side for 2 minutes.

Meanwhile, mix together all the ingredients for the dipping sauce and have it ready.

Put the cooked frittatas on a large serving plate with a dish of dipping sauce and serve.

fresh from the sea

Surrounded by water, Japanese cooks make full and extensive use of the sea's riches in their daily cooking. It is impossible to separate fish from Japanese cuisine. Visitors to Japan can witness the fondness for fish and seafood at the capital's central wholesale food market in Tsukiji and its surrounding neighborhood. For six days a week, under one roof, 800 wholesale traders buy and sell over 500 kinds of some 2,000 tons of fresh, frozen, or processed fish and seafood, generating ¥2 billion (more than 17.5 million dollars) worth of business a day. Tsukiji's pre-eminence in the world fish business sums up Japan's fondness for fish—the nation is the world's largest importer of fish and seafood, accounting for half of the global 31.5 billion dollar trade.

Japanese cooks go shopping every day to buy the freshest fish of the season. These days, however, we inevitably go to the supermarket; there we can find almost any type of fish, already-filleted throughout the year. I used to be highly dogmatic about fish farming and tried to eat only wild fish—now I humbly eat my words. Sustainable organic fish farming holds the key to the future.

There is no doubt that eating fish is healthy—it has high-quality protein that is easier to digest than that of meat or poultry. Fish is rich in vitamins including vitamin A, which benefits eyesight and helps improve the body's natural immune system. Mackerel, herring and plaice are particularly high in vitamin B2 and niacin that helps maintain healthy eyesight, skin, and the function of digestive organs. Both fish and shellfish are rich in calcium, iron and other minerals. But the most striking argument for eating more fish lies in the latest findings of an Anglo-American research project on omega-3 fatty acid found in fish. The research shows that the children of mothers who ate food with a low omega-3 content during their pregnancies had a lower IQ than their peers, found normal social relations harder to deal with, and lacked fine-tuned physical co-ordination. Nobody is suggesting that fixing maternal nutrition now would cure bad behavior in the future and result in a nation of well-coordinated geniuses, but there is increasing evidence that it would help.

In this book, I would like to demystify the Japanese way with fish and demonstrate that it is not all raw sashimi and sushi—far from it. We have so many different means of cooking fish to suit every occasion, ability and, above all, each of the four seasons. I hope to inspire you to cook more fish for your family and friends.

Grilled sweet miso-marinated cod

Miso is one of the essential ingredients in Japanese cooking. Japanese home cooks make a wide use of miso not only for its nutritional and health benefits but also for its distinctive taste and aroma. It is healthy and tasty. The marinating transfers miso's aroma and flavor and increases the natural umami found in the fish. Although the traditional recipe calls for Saikyo miso, which is a light-colored mild miso paste produced in the Kyoto area, you can use any light-colored miso.

4 cod or hake fillets, each
weighing 4 ounces
4 teaspoons pickled ginger for
garnish (optional)

for the sweet miso marinade
3/4 cup sake
1/2 cup granulated sugar
1 tablespoon light-colored miso
paste

For the sweet miso marinade, put the sake in a saucepan and bring to a boil to burn off its alcohol for a few minutes, then turn off the heat. Add the sugar and stir to dissolve. Stir in the miso paste until well blended. Set aside to cool. Transfer the miso marinade to a covered, flat-bottomed food container and cover the fish fillets with the marinade. Refrigerate overnight.

Preheat the broiler. Wipe the fillets with your fingers or kitchen paper. Do not wash them as it will spoil the taste and aroma. The fish should feel firmer. Place the fillets under the broiler for 5–7 minutes until golden and then turn over and broil the other side for 3–5 minutes. Keep an eye on the fish as it burns very easily. Garnish with sushi ginger, if desired, and serve.

Cook's tip

The famous Japanese restaurant chain Nobu brought this traditional dish into the limelight using black cod fillet, which is not actually related to cod. You can use any white fish. The miso marinade can be refrigerated and reused once or twice—bring to a boil to reheat. This will evaporate any excess liquid and destroy any bacteria. Do not marinate for longer than overnight as over-marinating makes the fish dry and tough, with an overpowering taste of miso. Simply serve with steamed green beans or, in the summer, a few sprigs of watercress.

Seared tuna steak with daikon dressing

Tuna is Japan's number one favorite fish. Tsukiji fish market in Tokyo alone trades over 2,000 tunas, fresh or frozen, daily and nearly half of the wholesale traders specialize in tuna. Although the nation's favorite way of eating tuna is raw in sashimi or sushi, quickly searing the outside is probably less scary for the home cook.

4 tuna steaks, each weighing
   about 4 ounces and cut 1¼
   inches thick
1 tablespoon vegetable oil
handful of arugula leaves
8 chives, finely chopped

for the marinade
⅓ cup soy sauce
3 tablespoons sake
2 tablespoons rice vinegar
1 garlic clove, minced

for the daikon dressing
¼ cup grated daikon
   (Japanese white radish)
¼ cup soy sauce
4 teaspoons lemon juice

Mix together all the ingredients for the marinade. Marinate the tuna steaks in it, turning once or twice, for at least 30 minutes. Remove the steaks from the marinade and pat them dry with paper towels.

Heat a heavy skillet or, better yet, a griddle pan over moderate heat. Brush the steaks with vegetable oil. Cook one side for 2 minutes, then turn and cook the other side for 1 to 2 minutes, until tuna is browned on the outside but still rare in the center.

Meanwhile, for the daikon dressing, mix the daikon with the soy sauce and lemon juice.

Transfer the steaks to individual serving plates and arrange the dressing and a few arugula leaves on them. Garnish with the chopped chives and serve.

Cook's tip
Tuna's robust taste needs something to counterbalance it, and I personally find buttery avocado a very good partner.

Simmered sardines in ginger vinegar

Some of you may have noticed by now that I use a lot of vinegar in cooking. Vinegar is a tasty and healthy ingredient with a wide range of culinary uses. It takes away the fishy aroma of sardines and it tenderizes meat, making it easier to digest.

8 fresh sardines

1 (1½-inch) piece of fresh
  ginger, peeled

1 red chile pepper
  (serrano or jalapeño)

²/₃ cup rice vinegar

¹/₃ cup sake

5 tablespoons soy sauce

2 tablespoons mirin

1 tablespoon sugar

heaping ¼ cup dried wakame
  seaweed

1 sheet of parchment paper cut
  the same size as the
  saucepan and punctured with
  a few small holes

Remove all the fish scales by scraping the blade of a kitchen knife from the tail end to the head. Remove the heads and gut the fish, or ask your fish store to do this for you. Rinse them under cold running water and pat dry with paper towels. Cut the ginger into small matchstick-sized pieces.

Put the sardines in a large shallow saucepan and add the ginger, chile, rice vinegar, sake, soy sauce, mirin, and sugar. Bring to a boil over a moderate heat and then reduce the heat to low as soon as the liquid begins to boil. Simmer, using the parchment paper as a lid that sits directly on the liquid, for 30 minutes.

Meanwhile, soak the dried wakame seaweed in a large bowl of water for 10 minutes or until soft. Drain, chop it coarsely and set aside.

Transfer the sardines to a large serving dish, arrange the ginger pieces over them and drizzle with a few tablespoons of the cooking juices. Add the wakame and serve.

Cook's tip

Serve with steamed or lightly boiled broccoli, cauliflower, and carrots.

Salt salmon flakes

In Japan, salmon is rarely eaten fresh; instead, it is salted. A slice of grilled salt salmon is one of the most popular dishes at breakfast, lunch, and dinner; in other words, at any time. All my grandmothers used to make their own salt salmon and yellowtail for the New Year holidays when fish markets were closed. I always sensed that another year was drawing to an end and a New Year was approaching when I saw a few big fish hanging under the eaves of the house. I wonder how a little bit of salt and cold winter wind could have made the fish so tasty that the flavor is still imprinted on my taste buds.

Salt is one of the most important ingredients in Japanese cooking. We use salt to flavor, season, preserve, dehydrate, anti-oxidize, and to freshen up the colors of food, so it is a pity that this remarkable ingredient is often misunderstood and seen as a villain of the modern healthy lifestyle. Of course, too much salt on anything is bad for you. But the real villain is what I call "hidden salt", present in many processed foods, over which you have no control. But in your own kitchen you are in control—this is one of the reasons why I love cooking.

I resumed the family tradition of preparing salt salmon last winter when I was writing this book. Since then there have always been a few slices of salt salmon and a jar of salmon flakes in my refrigerator, so that I can make a tasty meal at a moment's notice or at the first rumbling of my tummy. They are also useful for adding to salads or pasta sauces.

How to make salt salmon

1 whole side of fresh organic
*   salmon fillet, skin on*
2 tablespoons sea salt

Choose a fresh organic salmon. Selecting is always easier if you can see the whole fish, as it gives you more clues to its freshness. Pick one with clear bright eyes, glistening silver skin, and bright gills. Above all, it should not smell fishy; fresh fish should smell of the sea but not have an unpleasant odor. Get your fishmerchant to fillet the salmon if you can't do it yourself. (Remember: there is no shame in asking—in fact, a good fishmerchant will be delighted to do it for you.) Put the fillet on a clean work surface and sprinkle 1 tablespoon of salt over one side, then do the same on the other. Wrap it with triple-layered paper towels and place it on a plastic tray lined with a few sheets of newspaper; do not cover it. Refrigerate for 4–5 days.

Cook's tip

Salt salmon will keep for about 7 days in the refrigerator. Slice and grill it as needed.
The method works equally well with other fish such as yellowtail, sea bream (refrigerate for only 2–3 days), and mackerel (for 1–2 days).

How to make salt salmon flakes

12 ounces salt salmon
  (see page 68)
3 tablespoons sake
1 tablespoon soy sauce

Boil the salt salmon fillets for 10 minutes. Drain and let them cool enough to handle. Remove the skin and, with your hands, flake them. Put a nonstick skillet over a moderate heat and add the fish flakes. Stir rapidly with either two pairs of chopsticks or a wooden egg whisk to fluff the fish. Add the sake and soy sauce and continue to cook until nearly all the liquid has evaporated. Let it cool to room temperature before transferring to a glass jar to store in the refrigerator.

The salt salmon flakes work wonderfully well with cooked soba or udon noodles and pasta. They also make a good salad topping. The more traditional way is to serve them on top of freshly cooked rice.

Grilled yuzu-marinated turbot (brill) with bell peppers

Yuzu is a highly aromatic Japanese citrus fruit used only in cooking. Outside Japan the juice is available in bottles, but lime juice makes a good substitute.

4 turbot slices cut about 3/4-inch
  thick, each weighing about
  4 ounces
1 green bell pepper, quartered
1 red bell pepper, quartered
1 yellow bell pepper, quartered
1 tablespoon vegetable oil

for the yuzu marinade
1/4 cup light soy sauce
1/4 cup sake
2 tablespoons yuzu juice or
  lime juice
2 tablespoons mirin

Using the tip of a sharp knife, make a criss-cross slash marks on both sides of each fish slice to encourage the marinade to penetrate. Mix the yuzu marinade ingredients in a shallow dish, add the fish and marinate for 30 minutes, turning once or twice.

Preheat the broiler and line a baking sheet with aluminum foil. Brush the quartered bell peppers with the oil. Place the fish and bell peppers on the baking sheet and broil 4–6 inches from the heat for 6–8 minutes on one side. Brush the fish with more marinade and turn to cook the other side for 5–7 minutes or until the fish is lightly browned on the outside and just white throughout. Remove the bell peppers and keep them warm as they cook faster than the fish. Serve the fish with the bell peppers.

Aromatic steamed salmon with shallots and broccoli

I am greatly encouraged by the rising public criticism of intensive fish farming. People have realized that the price of salmon is not the only thing being brought down by intensive fish farming, but also the quality of the fish at an immeasurable cost to the environment. There is a growing number of organic salmon farms producing chemical-free fish in more environmentally friendly surroundings. Sustainable organic fish farming must surely hold the key to the future.

1 pound organic salmon fillet

2 shallots

4 ounces broccoli

2 tablespoons cornstarch

for the aromatic seasoning

6 tablespoons soy sauce

¹⁄₄ cup sake

1 tablespoon Asian sesame oil

2 teaspoons juice from grated
   fresh ginger

freshly ground black pepper

Cut the salmon into 1¹⁄₄-inch chunks and put them in a bowl.

Mix together all the ingredients for the aromatic seasoning and pour the mixture over the salmon. Stir to ensure that each salmon piece is coated with the mixture and set aside for 15 minutes.

Cut the shallots and the broccoli into bite-sized pieces.

Pat the salmon dry with paper towels and dust it with cornstarch. Put the vegetables and salmon in a heat-resistant bowl, place in a steamer basket and steam, covered, for 15–18 minutes or until salmon is just opaque throughout. Serve on warmed plates drizzled with the cooking juices .

Cook's tip

Why not serve this with plain boiled or mashed potatoes to soak up all the tasty cooking juices?

Oven-baked parcels of konbu-flavored flounder

This is a highly sophisticated and delicious way of presenting a subtle-flavored fish like plaice or sole with surprisingly little cooking. Umami, found in abundance in konbu (kelp seaweed), transfers to, and intensifies, the delicious taste of the fish, which is wrapped in a parcel so that no taste and flavor is lost. The konbu is made into bows for visual effect.

4 sheets of konbu (kelp
*   seaweed), big enough to wrap*
*   each fish fillet*
¹/₂ teaspoon salt
4 flounder fillets, each
*   weighing about 4 ounces*
1 teaspoon vegetable oil
¹/₄ cup sake
1 lime or lemon, cut into
*   4 wedges*
4 (12-inch) squares of
*   aluminum foil*

Cover the konbu sheets with a clean damp tea cloth for 10 minutes to soften.

Meanwhile, sprinkle salt on the fish fillets and set aside for 5–10 minutes. Take the softened konbu sheets and pat dry with paper towels. Use one konbu sheet to wrap each fillet. Cover tightly with plastic wrap and refrigerate for 2–3 hours.

Preheat the oven to 325°F. Unwrap the fillets from the konbu—reserve one sheet and discard the rest.

Cut four ribbons (¹/₂ inch wide x 3¹/₂ inches long) from the reserved sheet of konbu and tie a knot in the middle of each ribbon. Lightly brush the centerpart of each aluminum foil sheet with vegetable oil and place the fillets on them, add the konbu knots and pour the sake over the top. Bring up the edges of the foil to make parcels. Put the parcels on a baking sheet and place in the middle of the oven to bake for 10–15 minutes. Lay each parcel, unopened, on a plate and serve with a lime or lemon wedge.

Cook's tip

You can use any flat fish for this recipe. If the fish is fresh sashimi quality, just do the konbu marinade and serve raw as sashimi.

This recipe requires something delicate to accompany it. Why not try steamed green beans or bok choy?

Pan-sautéd marlin with citrus teriyaki sauce

The marlin is a large handsome fish with an impressive bill. Its flesh is a pinkish-orange color. It is a healthy fish, high in protein and low in fat, but the most notable health-giving element it contains is potassium, which helps prevent high blood pressure.

4 marlin steaks, each
   weighing about 4 ounces
1 tablespoon all-purpose flour
7 ounces shimeji mushrooms
2 tablespoons vegetable oil
²/₃ cup water
4 ounces broccoli, cut into
   bite-sized chunks
pinch of shichimi togarashi
   (Japanese seven-spice
   seasoning)

for the citrus teriyaki sauce
2 tablespoons medium-colored
   miso paste
2 tablespoons sake
1¹/₂ tablespoons granulated
   sugar
1 tablespoon soy sauce
1 tablespoon lime juice

Lightly dust the marlin steaks with the flour. Divide the shimeji mushrooms into four equal portions. Heat a skillet over a moderate heat and add the vegetable oil. Quickly sauté the marlin steaks on both sides and set them aside. Add the water to the pan with the mushrooms and broccoli and cook for 3–4 minutes.

Mix together all the ingredients for the citrus teriyaki sauce and have it ready.

Remove the vegetables from the pan with a slotted spoon and keep warm. Add the citrus teriyaki sauce to the pan and return the marlin steaks to cook until the liquid has reduced by about 20 per cent. Arrange the fish on individual serving plates, add the vegetables and drizzle over some of the cooking sauce. Garnish with shichimi togarashi and serve.

Japanese-style sea bass carpaccio

In Japan, sea bass is known as shusse uo, meaning "success fish" because it changes its name as it grows bigger. Sea bass is valued for its firm white flesh and good taste. You need sashimi-quality fresh wild sea bass for this recipe and there is no cooking involved.

7 ounces sashimi-quality wild sea bass fillet, skin removed

1/2 teaspoon salt

2 tablespoons sake

2 tablespoons rice vinegar

1 tablespoon lime juice

1 vine-ripened tomato, seeded and finely chopped

8 chives, finely chopped

for the wasabi miso sauce

2 tablespoons soy sauce

2 tablespoons water

1 tablespoon medium-colored miso paste

1 teaspoon wasabi powder

1/2 teaspoon sugar

freshly ground black pepper

With a sharp knife, slice the sea bass fillet as thinly as possible. You will find it easier if you wrap the fillet with plastic wrap and freeze it for 10–15 minutes. Lay the slices on a shallow dish and sprinkle with the salt. Pour the sake, vinegar, and lime juice over the top and refrigerate, covered, for 1–2 hours.

Meanwhile, for the wasabi miso sauce, mix all the ingredients together in a bowl and set aside.

Transfer the fish slices onto four individual serving plates. Drizzle with the prepared wasabi miso sauce, garnish with the chopped tomato and chives, and serve.

Cook's tip

You can try this recipe with other white fish, such as sea bream, flounder or halibut. But make sure the fish is sashimi-quality—in other words, really fresh.
Serve with a fresh salad and Japanese dressing (see page 169).

New sashimi of sea bream with hot oil

If tuna is the heavyweight champion fish in the Japanese kitchen, sea bream or snapper is the royal king. Sea bream is a handsome-looking fish with firm pinkish-white flesh and a wonderful flavor. It is also prized as favorable—it adorns every celebratory table because its Japanese name, tai, is a pun on the Japanese word for auspicious. The presence of this fish immediately lights up a table. It is low in fat, high in protein, and easy to digest, making it suitable for all ages. This is an easy-to-do, but highly dramatic recipe with an impressive taste and flavor.

8 ounces sashimi-quality sea
bream fillet, skin removed
1/3 teaspoon salt
1–2 garlic cloves, minced
2 tablespoons lemon juice
1 tablespoon light soy sauce
1 tablespoon uncooked
rice grains
1/2 teaspoon shichimi togarashi
(Japanese seven-spice
seasoning)

for the hot oil
2 tablespoons grapeseed oil
1 teaspoon Asian sesame oil

You will find it easier to cut the fish into thin slices if it is wrapped in plastic wrap and frozen for 10–15 minutes. Unwrap and cut the fish fillet into thin slices and arrange on a large serving plate. Sprinkle with the salt and rub the grated garlic on each slice.

Pour the lemon juice over the top and wait a few minutes for the fish slices to "cook" (the color of the fish turns from translucent to white opaque), then drizzle with soy sauce.

Meanwhile, toast the rice in a dry, hot skillet, stirring, until lightly browned. Grind and set aside.

In a ladle, heat the grapeseed oil and sesame oil until almost smoking. Pour the hot oil mixture over the fish slices. This is a rather dramatic moment, creating a sizzling noise and splashing of oil that semicooks the fish. Take care not to burn yourself with the hot oil. Garnish with shichimi togarashi and the ground rice and serve at once.

Cook's tip

If you are preparing this in advance, proceed up to the stage where you heat the oil, cover the plate with plastic wrap and keep refrigerated.
The subtle and gentle flavors of young snow peas or steamed green beans make good partners for this dish.

Skate wing with wasabi

I first came across the delights of skate wings in England. They are delicious and succulent and easy to eat—even for those who are not generally comfortable when dealing with fish on the plate. Skate can sometimes smell slightly of ammonia, which can be off-putting for some, so I have come up with a recipe that solves this minor problem with a delicious Japanese twist!

2 red onions

4 skate wings, each weighing about 4 ounces

¹/₄ cup all-purpose flour

¹/₄ cup vegetable oil

for the cooking liquid

4 heaping tablespoons drained capers

2 tablespoons sake

2 tablespoons rice vinegar

2 teaspoons wasabi powder

Slice the onions as thinly as possible and soak in a bowl of cold water—this removes any strong onion smell and refreshes them.

Wipe the skate wings clean and dust with flour. Heat a large skillet over a high heat and add the vegetable oil. Fry the skate wings for 3–5 minutes on each side or until they are golden brown and crisp on the outside. Reduce the heat to low.

In a small bowl, mix together all the ingredients for the cooking liquid. Pour it over the skate wings and simmer for 1–2 minutes.

Drain the onion slices. Put the skate wings on individual serving plates, drizzle with the cooking liquid, arrange the drained onion slices on top, and serve.

Cook's tip

Serve with Japanese new potato salad (see page 44) or tomato and tofu salad (see page 40).

Hot-and-sour vinegar-pickled shrimp

Here is an easy, nothing-to-do-at-the-last-minute recipe with plenty of flavor. Both rice vinegar and umeboshi (pickled plums) pickle and preserve the shrimp and the vegetables while you sleep. In an ideal world, the shrimp should be left at least 24 hours to allow the flavors to develop. A tablespoon of wasabi may sound fiery-hot, but provides merely an undertone of lively heat.

12 cooked jumbo shrimp
1 red bell pepper, seeded and
sliced lengthwise into
thin strips
1 yellow bell pepper, seeded and
sliced lengthwise into
thin strips
1 small red onion, thinly sliced
1 lime, thinly sliced
cilantro sprigs

for the pickling liquid
¼ cup rice vinegar
¼ cup yuzu juice or lime juice
2 tablespoons light soy sauce
2 umeboshi (pickled plums),
mashed
1 tablespoon sugar
1 tablespoon wasabi powder,
mixed with 2 tablespoons
water

Remove the shells and heads of the shrimp but leave the tails on, as they look attractive. Run the tip of a small knife along the back of each prawn and remove the black vein that sometimes runs from head to tail. Place the shrimp, sliced peppers, onion, and lime in a shallow glass or plastic container with a lid.

Mix together all the ingredients for the pickling liquid and pour over the shrimp. Cover the container and refrigerate for at least 24 hours—give the contents occasional shakes or stir from time to time to ensure even pickling.

Serve the shrimp and the vegetables with sprigs of cilantro and a generous amount of the pickling juice.

Cook's tip
Serve with a big bowl of green salad with Japanese salad dressing (see page 169).

Oyster congee

Oysters are delicious, health-giving seafood, rich in minerals and B vitamins. Like many children, I did not like raw oysters, so my mother used to cook them in soupy rice for my late night snack when I stayed up to study for exams. A steaming bowl of oyster congee made late-night studying a little more bearable. It is quick to make, deliciously comforting, and very easy to digest.

about 12 freshly shucked oysters
with their liquor (about 7
ounces without shells)
1 tablespoon lime juice
1 postcard-sized piece of konbu
(kelp seaweed)
2¹/₂ cups water
2¹/₂ cups cold cooked rice
2 tablespoons light soy sauce
handful of watercress, chopped
2 teaspoons grated fresh ginger
¹/₂ sheet of nori (dried seaweed),
torn into small pieces

Put the oysters and their liquor in a bowl. Drizzle with lime juice and set aside. Put the konbu and the water in a heavy saucepan and let it come to a boil over a moderate heat. When the konbu floats to the surface, add the oysters and cook 1 minute. Remove with a slotted spoon or small sieve, and set them aside. Reduce the heat to low and add the rice and soy sauce; simmer for 10 minutes. Gently stir in the oysters and watercress.

Garnish each serving with a pinch of grated ginger and sprinkle the nori pieces over the top.

Cook's tip
Serve with cauliflower miso gratin (see page 56), spicy stir-fried spinach with pancetta (page 58) or Pot au feu of Chinese cabbage and bacon (page 60) for that really comforting effect.

Crabmeat, spinach, and shimeji ohitashi

There is no equivalent dish for *ohitashi* in Western cooking. The best way to describe it is a salad in broth. It can be served warm in the winter and chilled in the summer.

8 ounces baby spinach leaves
4 ounces shimeji mushrooms
4 ounces crabmeat

for the ohitashi broth
1³/₄ cups dashi stock
(see pages 16–17)
3 tablespoons light soy sauce
1¹/₂ tablespoons sake

Blanch the spinach in boiling water and drain well. Discard the base of the shimeji mushrooms and separate them. For the broth, mix together the dashi, soy sauce, and sake in a saucepan. Add the shimeji mushrooms and bring to a boil over a moderate heat. Reduce the heat to low and simmer for 2 minutes; turn off the heat and set aside to cool for 5–10 minutes. When the broth has cooled to body temperature add the crabmeat and spinach and stir gently to mix. Divide the mixture into four equal portions and serve warm.

Cook's tip
This recipe has three of my favorite winter ingredients, but you can experiment with your own favorites. In the spring, try an ohitashi of asparagus with shrimp.

Seared scallops with sweet-and-sour umeboshi sauce

Scallops are rich in protein, low in calories, and contain vitamin B2, which metabolizes sugar and fat, but the most notable nutrient is taurine that prevents deterioration of the eyesight and helps restore tired optic nerves. They have the second highest zinc content among seafood, after oysters. It is said that you use up more zinc if you are stressed. But I am sure this recipe causes you no stress, as it is very simple with a delicious result.

12 large, plump sea scallops

1/2 teaspoon salt

1 tablespoon vegetable oil

1 bunch of watercress, trimmed

for the umeboshi sauce

1/4 cup granulated sugar

11/2 tablespoons water

2 tablespoons rice vinegar

1 tablespoon soy sauce

2 tablespoons umeboshi purée
  (pickled plums sold in tubes)

Slice the scallops horizontally in half, put them on a plate and sprinkle with salt.

For the sauce, mix the sugar and the 11/2 tablespoons water in a small saucepan and let it come to a boil over a moderate heat. Add the vinegar and soy sauce, then lower the heat and simmer for 5 minutes or until the sauce is reduced to a syrupy thickness. Remove from the heat, add the umeboshi purée and stir to dissolve. Set aside to cool.

Meanwhile, heat a griddle pan over high heat. Brush the scallops with oil and sear for 1–2 minutes on each side.

Divide the watercress into four equal portions and arrange each portion on a serving plate. Put six scallop slices on to each serving and drizzle the sauce over the top to serve.

Cook's tip

You can buy umeboshi purée in the supermarket. It is umeboshi ready mashed and puréed. Serve with warm bean sprout salad with crispy garlic (page 56) or green salad with Japanese salad dressing (see page 169).

Clams in green vinegar sauce with somen noodles

This is a refreshing pasta sauce with clams and wakame seaweed. It is best served chilled with either fine somen noodles or soba noodles.

1 pound clams, scrubbed clean

3/4 cup dry white wine

1/2 teaspoon salt

pinch of ground pepper

8 ounces dried somen noodles

1 large cucumber, peeled

1 tablespoon dried wakame
   seaweed, soaked in water

8 ounces seedless green grapes,
   halved

a few sprigs flat-leaf parsley,
   coarsely chopped (optional)

for the vinegar sauce

1/2 cup rice vinegar

2 tablespoons water

2 tablespoons soy sauce

2 tablespoons sugar

Put the clams in a saucepan with the wine, salt, and pepper. Cover and bring to a boil. Steam for 5 minutes or until all the shells have opened, shaking the saucepan continuously. Turn off the heat, remove the lid to let cool enough to remove the shells and reserve the clams. Reserve a few clams in their shells for garnish. Meanwhile, cook the somen noodles as described on the package and let them drain in a colander.

Grate the cucumber and squeeze it to remove excess water. Drain the wakame and chop it coarsely. Put the clams, cucumber, grapes, and wakame pieces in a large bowl. Mix together all the ingredients for the vinegar sauce and stir into the clam and cucumber mixture. Add the cooked noodles and divide into four equal portions. Garnish with the chopped parsley and serve.

Cook's tip

If you are serving this chilled, refrigerate the cucumber mixture, covered with plastic wrap, before adding the noodles. Do not refrigerate the noodles as they will stick together.

Stir-fry of squid with green and red bell peppers

There are many varieties of squid or cuttle fish used in Japanese cooking. Each variety has its most suitable way of being prepared but, in general, squid is prone to become tough and chewy when cooked, so it is best to cook it very fast or not at all. Flash stir-frying is therefore an ideal method.

1 average-sized squid, weighing about 1 pound

1 green bell pepper

1 red bell pepper

1 tablespoon vegetable oil

1 garlic clove, peeled and cut into matchstick-sized pieces

½ large red chile (serrano or jalapeño), finely chopped

2 tablespoons sake

1 teaspoon Asian sesame oil

1 teaspoon salt

½ teaspoon rice vinegar

To prepare the squid, pull off the tentacles to remove the innards. Carefully remove the ink sac, which is attached above the eyes, and discard. Rub a clean damp cloth over the body to peel off the skin. Remove the cartlidge from the body part. Tear off the fins and, again with the damp cloth, remove the skin from the body. Slice open the body and make shallow criss-cross slash marks with the tip of a sharp knife all over the body and fins to stop them from curling when heated. Cut the body and fins into large postage stamp-sized pieces. Cut the tentacles into 2–3 pieces.

Seed the bell peppers and cut them into the same-sized pieces as the squid.

Heat a wok or a skillet over a moderate/high heat and add the vegetable oil. Add the garlic pieces to infuse the oil and then quickly stir-fry the squid, adding the sake as it fries. Remove the garlic and squid with a large spoon. Add the sesame oil, peppers, and chile and stir-fry for 2–3 minutes and then return the garlic and squid. Add the vinegar. Adjust the seasoning with salt, and toss and stir. Take it off the heat, transfer the mixture onto a large serving dish and serve immediately.

Cook's tip

This is a very colorful main course dish, which can be served with new potatoes in spring and summer and roasted sweet potatoes with soy honey glaze (see page 54) or roast pumpkin and garlic mash (page 57) in colder months.

Wakame and yam salad

Japanese people regard seaweeds as ocean vegetables and use over fifty varieties of them in their cuisine. Wakame is very healthy and contains no calories; it is also full of calcium, minerals, and iodine. It prevents high blood pressure, hardening of the arteries, is rich in edible fiber to prevent constipation, and its high iodine content helps the body's natural immunity. Outside Japan, wakame is available either in dried or salted forms, both of which require soaking in water before use.

3/4 *ounce dried wakame*

6 *ounces yam, peeled and*
   thinly sliced

3 *tablespoons rice vinegar*

1 *package cress*

handful of bonito fish flakes

3 *tablespoons soy sauce*

2 *tablespoons rice vinegar*

Soak the dried wakame in water for 10–15 minutes to soften. Drain well. Soak the yam pieces in a bowl of water with the rice vinegar for 10–15 minutes and drain.

Put the wakame, yam, cress, and bonito fish flakes in a salad bowl. Drizzle with the soy sauce and rice vinegar. Toss to coat and serve.

Cook's tip

This makes an excellent starter or an accompanying side salad for any main course dishes.

poultry and eggs

Cooking with meat and poultry is not the first thing that comes to mind when you think of Japanese food. Although young Japanese people are eating more meat and poultry than their parents' or grandparents' generations, the amount is still small compared to the intake of other developed nations. In Japanese cooking, there is no equivalent of cooking a large roast or a whole chicken or turkey. Meat and poultry are butchered differently—generally they are sold in smaller, thinner cuts to suit the Japanese cooking style and eating with chopsticks.

Chicken returned to the Japanese table in the mid-nineteenth century after a 1,200-year absence and quickly gained popularity. In Japan today, chicken is eaten more than any other meat. Chicken is popular for its mild and leaner taste, its ability to partner with other foods and because it is less expensive than other meats, especially beef.

I am old enough to remember that in the early '60's there were shops in Japan that sold nothing but eggs. A dozen eggs neatly laid out in a box of sawdust was a precious gift in those days. Eggs were an important source of otherwise scarce animal protein.

Today both chicken and eggs are the most intensively farmed foods, and some of the cheapest food on the market. But at what cost, I wonder? I can't emphasize enough the importance of choosing the best-quality chickens and eggs in order to get the authentic, natural flavor and the enjoyment out of eating them. In Japanese cuisine you don't need large amounts of chicken or eggs, so you can afford to buy the best quality, and, ideally, support your local organic suppliers.

Japanese-style chicken burger with grated daikon

There are many dishes that the Japanese have "borrowed" from other cuisines and adapted to suit their food culture, and this is a good example. The good news is that this is one burger that doesn't leave you worrying about your waistline.

4 ounces firm cotton tofu, well drained (see page 110)

8 ounces ground chicken

2 shallots, finely chopped

1 garlic clove, minced

2 teaspoons peeled and grated fresh ginger

1 small free-range egg, lightly beaten

1 tablespoon cornstarch

salt and black pepper

8 ounces daikon (Japanese white radish), peeled and grated

juice of 1/2 lemon

2 tablespoons soy sauce

1 tablespoon vegetable oil

In a large mixing bowl, mash the tofu with a fork and drain off any excess water.

Mix together the chicken, shallots, garlic, ginger, egg, and cornstarch. Season with salt and pepper. Shape the mixture into four equal-sized patties about 1¹/₄-inches thick. Put them on a plate lined with paper towels, cover with plastic wrap and refrigerate for at least 2 hours to develop the flavors.

Meanwhile, grate the daikon and combine with the lemon juice and soy sauce.

Heat the vegetable oil in a large skillet over medium-high heat. Cook the burgers for 5 minutes on one side, then turn them over and cook 4 minutes, or until golden on the outside and white throughout but still juicy. Top each burger with a generous spoonful of the daikon mixture.

Cook's tip

Serve this recipe at your next barbecue with a green salad and the soba noodle salad with smoked salmon, salmon roe, and grated daikon on page 143.

Chicken yakitori

There is nothing so tempting as the aroma of grilled chicken wafting down the streets of Tokyo. Yakitori must be the nation's favorite bar snack. But you don't have to be an adult to enjoy these mouth-watering mini kebabs. I marinate the chicken to minimize cooking time, so the meat remains succulent and the aroma of the soy-basting sauce does not dissipate.

8 chicken tenders or small fillets

for the marinade
¼ cup soy sauce
¼ cup sake
¼ cup mirin
1–2 tablespoons sugar
shichimi togarashi (Japanese
*   seven-spice seasoning)*

8 bamboo skewers, soaked
*   in water*

Mix together all the ingredients for the marinade in a bowl. Add the chicken fillets and marinate for at least 2 hours.

Preheat the broiler to the highest heat and line a baking sheet with aluminum foil to catch the drips of marinade (and make clean up a lot easier). Thread the chicken onto bamboo skewers. Brush the remaining marinade over the kebabs, place on the baking sheet and grill for 5 minutes, then turn them over and grill for 2–3 minutes. Remove from the broiler, sprinkle on the shichimi togarashi and serve 2 skewers to each diner, either hot or at room temperature.

Cook's tip
Serve at a summer barbecue with Japanese new potato salad (see page 44) and green salad. It also makes a great appetizer or party food.

Sake-steamed chicken parcels with pak choi

Steam-cooking is a gentle way of applying heat to an ingredient. It is a particularly suitable method of cooking delicate-flavored ingredients such as chicken and vegetables. Be sure to get as good-quality chicken as possible because both the seasoning and cooking are simple, so the real flavor of the chicken comes through and there is no disguising poor quality ingredients.

4 boneless, skinless chicken
   breast halves
½ teaspoon sea salt
¼ cup sake
1 teaspoon vegetable oil
1 pak choi (bok choy), cut into
   bite-sized pieces
1 lime, quartered

4 (12-inch) squares of
   aluminum foil

Put the chicken in a bowl and rub with the salt; pour in the sake. Cover the bowl with plastic wrap and refrigerate for at least 2 hours—preferably longer—to let the sake tenderize the chicken.

Lightly oil the center of each aluminum foil square. Place the chicken breasts and pak choi on them and pour over the sake marinade. Make a parcel by pulling in the four corners of each sheet of foil, leaving enough space to let the steam circulate. Place the parcels in a large steamer basket and steam for 15–18 minutes over a moderate heat. If you are in any doubt about the cooking time, turn the heat off but leave the parcels in the steamer for another 5 minutes before serving. Place the parcels on individual plates and serve each with a lime quarter. Let your guests open their own parcels.

Cook's tip
This makes an excellent dinner or party dish—everyone enjoys opening a culinary parcel.

Soy-marinated roast chicken legs

Although you have to plan ahead and start the night before to let the full flavor develop and the chicken to tenderize, it is well worth the little extra effort. Try it once and I am sure you will agree.

4 chicken legs

1 tablespoon vegetable oil

1 teaspoon Asian sesame oil

for the marinade

1/3 cup soy sauce

3 tablespoons sake

3 tablespoons mirin

4 garlic cloves, peeled and crushed

2 tablespoons sugar

Make 3–4 incisions on each chicken leg across the muscle tendon to help the marinade penetrate. Put the chicken in a bowl, mix together all the marinade ingredients, and pour over the chicken. Marinate overnight in the refrigerator.

Preheat the oven to 375°F. Take the chicken legs out of the marinade and pat dry with paper towels. Mix the vegetable and sesame oils, brush the legs with them and roast for 25–30 minutes. Turn off the oven and leave the chicken inside until you are ready to serve. This way the chicken legs will be juicy and succulent.

Cook's tip

Why not serve with roasted vegetables of your choice and roasted sweet potato with soy honey glaze (see page 54)?

Chicken teriyaki with ginger and vinegar

I am a self-confessed vinegar addict—I use it for cooking, soaking my hands, cleaning the kitchen, and I even drink it as a nightcap. A dash of vinegar at the end of cooking highlights all the flavors of a dish—you don't need a single pinch of salt.

4 boneless chicken thighs, skin on

1/4 cup cornstarch

1 tablespoon vegetable oil

5 tablespoons teriyaki sauce (see page 167)

1 tablespoon peeled, grated fresh ginger

1 tablespoon rice vinegar

Place the chicken pieces skin-side down, make 3–4 incisions across the tendon of each one and dust with cornstarch. Heat the oil in a skillet and cook the chicken skin-side down over moderate heat for 5 minutes or until the skin becomes golden and crisp. Turn over and place a lid on the pan to steam for 4 minutes. Remove the lid and add the teriyaki sauce and grated ginger. Shake the pan to coat the chicken evenly with the sauce. Add the rice vinegar and cook 5 minutes longer, allowing the liquid to reduce slightly. Serve the chicken at once with the cooking juices.

Cook's tip

Serve with any vegetable of your choice; I like steamed broccoli, cauliflower, or green beans. Drizzle extra teriyaki sauce over the vegetables.

Crispy duck breast with tangerine sauce on watercress

This is a Japanese version of the famous French dish. The richness of the duck meat is well balanced with the bittersweet tangerine sauce and watercress. I am using just one duck breast for two servings because the breasts I buy from my village butcher are quite large and can easily supply two portions, but by all means adjust the amount to suit your appetite.

4 tangerines

2 duck breasts

2 tablespoons salt

vegetable oil

¼ cup sake

2 tablespoons soy sauce

1 small bunch watercress

Peel two of the tangerines and separate the segments. Remove the pith from each segment and set aside. Halve the other two tangerines, squeeze out the juice and reserve.

Using the tip of a very sharp knife, lightly score through the skin and fat of the duck breasts. Take care not to cut into the flesh. Rub salt into the skin and incisions—this helps release the fat during cooking and make the skin crisp.

Heat a skillet over a moderate heat and brush with oil. Place the breasts skin-side down and cook for 5–7 minutes to release the fat. Remove them from the pan. Discard the fat and return the pan to a high heat. Put the breasts skin-side up and cook for 2–3 minutes to seal. Turn it over and cook the other side for 5–6 minutes or until the skin becomes golden and crisp. Remove the breasts to a warmed plate to rest for a few minutes before cutting it into manageable slices. Turn down the heat to low/moderate and add the sake to the meat juices in the pan. When the sauce is bubbling, add the tangerine juice and soy sauce and bring it back to a boil.

Meanwhile, divide the watercress into equal portions and arrange the duck slices on top. Scatter some tangerine segments around them, pour the sauce over the top, and serve at once.

Cook's tip

This is a full-flavored rich main course dish, so serve it with plain-cooked soba noodles, if desired. Use a fork to twist the noodles into small mounds.

Japanese omelet with tomato and chives

A small amount of dashi broth makes an omelet light and succulent. For 1 egg, add 1 tablespoon of dashi, 1 teaspoon of sugar, and 1 teaspoon of light soy sauce. Sugar brings out the egg's umami and gives a light gloss to the surface. It helps to have a square omelet pan but it is not essential—to prove my point, an ordinary round omelet pan is used here.

3 free-range organic eggs,
lightly beaten
3 tablespoons dashi broth
(see pages 16–17)
1 tablespoon sugar
1 teaspoon light soy sauce
1 vine-ripened tomato, seeded and
finely chopped
6 chives, finely chopped
1 tablespoon vegetable oil

Mix together the eggs, broth, sugar, soy sauce, tomato, and chives. Soak some rolled-up paper towels with vegetable oil and have it ready. Heat an omelet pan over a moderate/ high heat and brush with the oiled paper. Drop a teaspoon of the egg mixture into the pan to test the temperature—listen for a "juwaaa" sound. Pour in about a quarter of the egg mixture and quickly rotate the pan to coat.

When the egg mixture begins to bubble up, gather the egg towards you from the far side of the pan, using a pair of chopsticks or a spatula. Re-oil the uncovered area of the pan with the oiled paper. Push the omelette to the far side, re-oil the uncovered area and pour in another quarter of the egg mixture. Repeat the process of gathering, moving, and re-oiling until all the egg mixture is used up.

Turn over the omelet to cook the underside. Transfer the omelet to a chopping board and place another straight-edged object against it to shape into a square. Cut into bite-sized pieces and serve.

Cook's tip
This recipe makes a light appetizer or party finger food.

Steamed savory egg custard

This is one of my favorite dishes, not only for its delectable taste but also for the smooth, silky sensation on your tongue. In summer I suggest making it in advance to serve chilled.

2 free-range organic eggs,
  lightly beaten
1¼ cups dashi broth
  (see pages 16–17)
1 teaspoon light soy sauce
4 teaspoons salmon roe
4 cooked medium shrimp,
  shelled
2 teaspoons sake

In a mixing bowl, mix the beaten eggs with the dashi and soy sauce. Strain the mixture into another bowl through a fine sieve. Divide the mixture into four equal portions and pour into heat-resistant cups—attractive tea/coffee cups are ideal.

Place the cups in a steamer basket and put a dishtowel under the lid to catch any condensation. The lid should be slightly ajar to let the steam escape. Steam for 2–4 minutes on a high heat, then reduce the heat to low and steam for another 8 minutes.

Mix the salmon roe with the sake—sake separates the roe and takes away the fishiness. Remove the cups from the steamer, garnish with the shrimp and roe and serve.

meat

It is no joke that eating beef was the most fashionable and politically correct thing to do in nineteenth-century Japan. In an attempt to modernize the country, the Japanese people aspired to and emulated every aspect of Western culture, including food. Emperor Meiji set a fine imperial example to the nation by eating beef for the first time in 1,200 years at the New Year banquet in 1872 and replacing the palace menus with French cuisine. For a nation that had abstained from eating beef and poultry for such a long time, the Japanese have quickly developed both a taste for and methods of rearing some of the finest-quality beef cattle in the world.

Kobe beef is internationally renowned for its quality and price. It is a brand name for a specially reared breed of Japanese beef cattle. In 1991 the Japanese domestic meat market was liberalized and cheap foreign imports flooded the country. Japanese beef farmers reorganized and decided to concentrate on high-value Japanese beef cattle rather than trying to compete against big and powerful producers like the U.S.A. and Australia. Names such as Kobe and Matsuzaka are among the most successful brands of beef.

Curiously, eating pork was never prohibited because pigs were kept for eating purposes only and never for agricultural labor nor for religious ceremonies. Lamb is a recent arrival at the Japanese table and probably will remain the least preferred type of meat because of its distinctive taste and smell.

Today the Japanese are eating eight times more meat than fifty years ago and now animal protein accounts for about a half of their total protein intake, though it is still small compared to that of Westerners. This is a huge increase and bound to affect the nation's state of health in generations to come.

Japanese ways of cooking with meat are distinctive; there is no tradition of roasting a large part of an animal. Meat is butchered and sold in smaller cuts and thin slices that are better suited to Japanese cooking and eating habits, which essentially involve surface heat and eating with chopsticks. Surprisingly small amounts of meat are required, since it is rarely cooked on its own. In Japan, while Buddhist principles, especially those of Zen Buddhism, are still revered and respected, vegetarianism is viewed with suspicion because it is not based on any religious belief and is seen as a fad without foundation.

The average Japanese person eats less than a quarter of the meat of his/her Western counterpart and probably feels quite happy about it. The little meat we eat, we certainly enjoy and make the most of. I have many friends who are so-called vegetarians and I love them all, though they do present me a challenge from time to time. I don't believe in cutting out anything from my diet—meat, fish, chocolate, bread, potatoes and so on—except wine during Lent, to remind me how to suffer.

Japanese-style beef steak

I believe that the Japanese way of eating with chopsticks has many health benefits. It forces you to eat more slowly than if you were using a knife and fork or a spoon, so that you chew for a longer time and get more of the digestive juices flowing. This makes the food easier to digest and so is kinder to your digestive system. With chopsticks, you can pick up only a smaller amount at a time, so each mouthful is smaller. Slower eating and longer chewing also mean you eat less. In this recipe, fillet steaks are served in bite-sized pieces, designed to be eaten with chopsticks. The meat is cooked with a modest amount of ginger and garlic-infused oil, adding more flavor.

4 beef fillet steaks, each
    weighing 4–5 ounces
salt and black pepper
¼ cup vegetable oil
4 ounces fresh ginger,
    peeled and thinly sliced
2 garlic cloves, thinly sliced
8 shiitake mushrooms,
    stalks removed
1 leek, trimmed and
    sliced diagonally
¼ cup sake
¼ cup soy sauce
2 tablespoons mirin
12 sprigs of watercress

Take the beef out of the fridge and let it come to room temperature (as cold meat is tough and takes longer to cook). Season with salt and pepper and set aside. Heat a large skillet over a moderate heat and add the vegetable oil. Lower the heat and fry the ginger and garlic slices until they are golden and crisp. You may find it easier to do this if you tilt the pan to gather the oil in a small area of the pan. With a slotted spoon, take out the ginger and garlic slices and leave them to drain on a piece of paper towel. Empty the oil into a small bowl to reserve.

Increase the heat to moderate/high, return the pan to the heat, and add 2 teaspoons of the oil. Working in batches if necessary, cook the shiitake mushrooms and leek. Remove the vegetables and keep them warm.

Add another teaspoon of the oil to the pan and brown the meat on both sides. Put a lid on the skillet to steam-cook for 1 minute. Take the meat out and keep it warm.

Add the sake, soy sauce, and mirin to the pan, let the sauce come to a boil and cook for 2 minutes to reduce.

Meanwhile, cut the meat into small bite-sized pieces and divide them between individual plates. Arrange the vegetables and watercress on the side, sprinkle the ginger and garlic slices on the meat, pour the sauce over the top and serve immediately.

Cook's tip

Serve with cooked green vegetables, such as broccoli, beans, or spinach. Try spring beans with sesame miso (see page 45).

Seared beef salad with watercress and grapefruit

This cooking method is called *tataki*, that literally means "to hit" or "to beat": you hit the meat with the palm of your hand to flatten and tenderize it. Traditionally the seared meat is plunged into iced water to stop further cooking and tighten. But recently I have used rice vinegar instead—the purpose of searing is not to cook the meat through but to burn off the fat and seal in the taste, whereas plunging in ice water will congeal the fat you are trying to get rid of.

8 ounces rump or sirloin steak

1 teaspoon vegetable oil

salt and black pepper

2 tablespoons rice vinegar

1 grapefruit, peeled and broken
    into segments

1 large bunch of watercress,
    trimmed

2 cups mixed baby lettuces

for the salad dressing

juice of 1 grapefruit

1/4 cup soy sauce

juice from a 3-inch piece
    fresh ginger (see page 54)

1 teaspoon sugar

Take the meat out of the refrigerator and let it come to room temperature (cold meat is tough and takes longer to cook). Brush the meat with the vegetable oil and rub with salt and pepper. Heat a griddle pan over a high heat and sear the meat on both sides. Place the meat on a chopping board. When cool enough to handle, use a sharp knife to slice the meat into 1/4-inch thick slices. Pour the rice vinegar over the top. Separate each slice and give it a light but firm slap with the palm of your hand.

Remove the thin membrane from each grapefruit segment. Put the watercress, arugula, baby lettuces, and grapefruit in a salad bowl and arrange the meat on top. Mix together the dressing ingredients, pour over the salad, toss, and serve.

Cook's tip

This recipe can work very well as a main course for a smart dinner party. You can change the combination of salad to suit your preference.

Japanese beefburger with shimeji mushrooms

In Japan, ground beef is rarely used on its own but combined with ground pork—the two varieties of meat complement each other in taste and nutrition and lighten the texture. In this recipe I also add finely chopped vegetables—a practice I began when my own children were very young and didn't always like eating certain vegetables, especially mushrooms. Now they are growing teenagers with the usual tastes for fast food, but I am happy and relieved that they still prefer this homemade hamburger.

for the hamburgers

8 ounces lean ground beef

8 ounces lean ground pork

1 medium onion, finely chopped

1/2 medium carrot, peeled
  and finely chopped

4 ounces portobello mushrooms,
  finely chopped

2 tablespoons cornstarch

1 free-range egg, lightly beaten

1/2 teaspoon salt

generous amount of freshly
  ground black pepper

1 tablespoon vegetable oil

for the mushroom sauce

2 tablespoons butter

2 garlic cloves, minced

4 ounces shiitake mushrooms,
  stems discarded and thinly sliced

about 5 ounces shimeji
  mushrooms, separated

handful of flat-leaf parsley,
  finely chopped

3 tablespoons sake

1 tablespoon soy sauce

1 teaspoon medium-colored
  miso paste

1/3 cup crème fraîche

In a large mixing bowl, combine the beef, pork, onion, carrot, portabello mushroom, cornstarch, egg, salt, and pepper. Mix well with clean hands. Divide the mixture into four equal portions and subdivide each quarter into three. I am allowing three mini burgers per person—small hamburgers cook faster and are easier to eat. Form twelve small, even-sized oval patties of about 1-inch thickness. Place them on a baking sheet in a single layer, cover, and set aside (up to 2 hours) in a cool part of your kitchen to let the flavors develop.

Heat a skillet over a moderate heat and add the vegetable oil. Cook the mini burgers in small batches for 1–2 minutes or until browned. Reduce the heat and cook for another 3 minutes on each side, until nicely browned on the outside and no longer pink on the inside. Remove them from the pan and cover to keep warm.

For the mushroom sauce, melt the butter in the pan and add the crushed garlic. Add the mushrooms and cook, stirring, for 3–4 minutes. Add the chopped parsley and season with sake, soy sauce, and miso. Stir in the crème fraîche. Let the sauce come to a boil, then cook for 2 minutes.

Place three mini burgers on each plate, spoon on the mushroom sauce and serve immediately.

Simmered beef with celery root

This recipe is an adaptation of a popular way of cooking meat with burdock; a long and thin aromatic root vegetable widely used in Japanese cooking. Burdock is, however, only available from Japanese grocery shops and does not keep fresh for a long time. So I came up with the idea of substituting celery root, and I think it works well.

1 pound celery root, cut into slices
  like thick wood shavings
3 tablespoons rice vinegar
1 tablespoon vegetable oil
1 pound chuck steak, thinly sliced
1 medium onion, thinly sliced
4 ounces fresh ginger, peeled and
  cut into matchstick-sized pieces
handful of cilantro, coarsely
  chopped

for the cooking liquid
$1/3$ cup sake
$1/3$ cup water
2 tablespoons sugar
$1/3$ cup mirin
$1/3$ cup soy sauce

Place celery root slices in a large bowl. Add rice vinegar and cold water to cover. Let sit 10 minutes—this refreshes the vegetable and keeps it crisp. Drain and transfer to a saucepan. Cover the celery root with plenty of fresh cold water and bring to a boil over a high heat. Reduce the heat to low after it reaches a boil. Cook for 5 minutes and drain.

Heat a wok or large skillet over moderate heat and add the vegetable oil. Add the beef and stir-fry for a few minutes or until it turns pale brown. Add all the ingredients for the cooking liquid in the order given and let it come to a boil. Add the celery root, onion, and ginger pieces. When the mixture returns to a boil, reduce the heat to low and simmer for 10 minutes. Turn off the heat and stir in the cilantro. Transfer to a large serving dish and serve.

Cook's tip
Try serving this on top of plain boiled rice as a one-bowl lunch or supper.

Pan-roasted pork tenderloin soused in soy

This is one of my favorite ways of cooking pork because it is fail-safe and has the added bonus of ending with a delicious, flavor-infused dressing.

12 ounces pork tenderloin
(fat trimmed)
1 teaspoon vegetable oil

**for the soy dressing/
"sousing liquid"**
3/4 cup soy sauce
3 tablespoons sake
3 tablespoons mirin
1 garlic clove, crushed
3 tablespoons yuzu juice or
lime juice

for the salad
2 bunches watercress
(about 7 ounces total)
1 medium cucumber, partly
peeled as desired, and
thinly sliced
1 package of alfalfa sprouts
8 small, vine-ripened tomatoes,
halved

Take the meat out of the refrigerator at least 30 minutes before you start cooking to let it come to room temperature (cold meat is tough and takes longer to cook). Cut the tenderloin in half lengthwise. Heat a nonstick skillet over high heat and add the vegetable oil. Brown the meat all over and reduce the heat to moderate/low, cover the pan with a lid and cook for 15 minutes.

Meanwhile, mix together all the ingredients for the soy dressing in a bowl. Add the meat to the dressing and let "souse" (marinate) at least 3 hours, but preferably overnight, to develop flavors.

Cut the pork into thin slices, arrange these on top of the salad, dress with the "sousing" liquid and serve.

Cook's tip
This recipe works very well as a one-dish lunch served with cooked soba noodles.

Teriyaki pork steak

Succulent tender pork is perfectly matched with nutty sweet teriyaki sauce. A dash of rice vinegar highlights the taste and flavors.

4 pork blade steaks, each
   weighing 4 ounces

¼ cup cornstarch

1 tablespoon vegetable oil

¼ cup rice vinegar

handful of watercress

for the teriyaki sauce

¼ cup sake

¼ cup mirin

2 tablespoons sugar

¼ cup soy sauce

1 (1½-inch) piece of fresh ginger,
   peeled and grated

Take the meat out of the refrigerator at least 30 minutes before cooking (cold meat is tough and takes longer to cook). Dust the steaks with the cornstarch. Heat a skillet over a moderate/low heat and add the vegetable oil. Sauté the steaks for 3 minutes on each side, then reduce the heat and cover the pan with a lid to steam-cook for 5 minutes.

Remove the lid and add all the ingredients for the teriyaki sauce. Shake the pan to coat the steaks evenly with the sauce and reduce it a little. Stir in the rice vinegar. Remove the steaks and cut them into bite-sized pieces. Arrange the meat on individual plates, drizzle with the sauce and serve with a garnish of watercress.

Cook's tip

This teriyaki cooking sauce works equally well with lamb chops. Serve with cauliflower miso gratin (see page 56) or leek and carrot mini fritattas (page 60).

Slow-cooked belly of pork

This is a real home-comfort slow food, taking two days to prepare what is often an underrated part of pork. The end result is simple but wholesome and tender. My grandmother used to say that you must be generous with your time because the pork will not be tender, but greasy, if you attempt to cook it in a hurry.

about 1 pound belly of pork

for the aromatic marinade

1 medium onion, halved

2 medium carrots,
    halved lengthwise

2 celery ribs

1 (1¹/₂-inch) piece of fresh ginger,
    peeled and gently bruised

2–3 garlic cloves, peeled and
    gently bruised

1 teaspoon black peppercorns

for the cooking liquid

4 dried shiitake mushrooms,
    soaked in ¹/₃ cup water*

1 ounce konbu (kelp seaweed)

²/₃ cup sake

¹/₂ cup light brown sugar

¹/₃ cup soy sauce

*reserve the soaking liquid

Put the pork with all the ingredients for the aromatic marinade in a large heavy saucepan and add enough water to cover everything. Put the saucepan over a moderate heat and bring to a boil, skimming off any scum that floats to the surface. Reduce the heat to low and let it simmer for 2 hours.

Discard the vegetables and let the whole saucepan cool to room temperature. Cover and refrigerate overnight. This is to solidify the fat and let the meat absorb all the flavor of the marinade.

Discard the solidified fat from the surface of the saucepan and reserve the soup. Cut the pork into 1-inch cubes and place in a single layer in a flameproof casserole or large saucepan. Cover the pork with a mixture consisting of two-thirds reserved soup and one third reserved water from the shiitake mushrooms. Place the konbu on top of the meat. Add the sake, sugar, and softened shiitake mushrooms and bring to a boil over a low/moderate heat. Let it simmer for 30 minutes before adding the soy sauce and then slow-cook for another 2 hours before serving.

Cook's tip

This makes a great winter warmer served with plenty of steamed vegetables and a dab of English mustard. It also goes particularly well with pot au feu of Chinese cabbage and bacon (see page 58).

Gyoza—pork dumplings

Dumplings are a typical example of how Japanese cooks adapt and develop a classic Chinese dish into something of their own. *Gyoza* are a very popular dish in Japan.

To make the dumpling mixture, discard the mushroom stems and finely chop the caps. Put all the ingredients for the dumplings in a bowl and mix well. Take one sheet of gyoza skin on your left palm and spoon 1 teaspoon of the dumpling mixture on to the center of the skin. Wet the edge of the skin with a pastry brush. Fold over one half of the skin to enclose the filling, then make a few pleats to seal. Put each dumpling on a baking sheet lined with parchment paper. Repeat the process to use up all the mixture.

Working in batches, heat a large skillet over a moderate heat, add the vegetable oil, fill the pan with gyoza; cook until brown. Turn them over. When they are browned, reduce the heat, pour in a glass of cold water and immediately put on a lid to steam-cook the dumplings. Remove the lid to let the liquid evaporate and then cook the dumplings for 3 minutes. Transfer them to a serving plate. Mix together all the ingredients for the dipping sauce and offer on the side.

for the dumpling mixture

2 dried shiitake mushrooms, soaked in warm water for 10–15 minutes

4 ounces Chinese, napa, or Savoy cabbage, finely chopped

4 ounces ground pork

2 garlic cloves, peeled and crushed

1 (1-inch) piece of ginger, peeled and finely grated

4 scallions, finely chopped

1 tablespoon cornstarch

1 teaspoon salt

2 teaspoons white pepper

48 sheets fresh/frozen gyoza skins (about 5 ounces)

vegetable oil for frying

for the dipping sauce

5 tablespoons soy sauce

3 tablespoons rice vinegar

2 teaspoons hot chile sesame oil

Cook's tip

The dumplings freeze very well and they can be cooked directly from frozen. Simply increase the cooking time and steam for a few minutes longer. The recipe works equally well with minced chicken or turkey instead of minced pork.

Try serving with warm bean sprout salad with crispy garlic (see page 57).

Pot-roasted rack of lamb with rice vinegar

Lamb is the most recent arrival at the Japanese table—in the early 1970's, after Britain's entry to the then Common Market, New Zealand mounted extensive marketing campaigns in Japan in an effort to find a new market for its lamb. It was a limited success. I love lamb and so does my family, but this is one area of cooking where I couldn't rely on my mother's or grandmothers' wisdom. So I created a new recipe with a Japanese twist and I hope you agree with me that it is rather yummy.

rack of lamb, providing
   2–3 lamb rib chops per person
2 tablespoons vegetable oil
1 large sprig of rosemary
1/3 cup rice vinegar
3 tablespoons mirin
3 tablespoons sake
1 pound spinach
1 cup canned cannellini or other
   white beans
3 tablespoons soy sauce
2 tablespoons cornstarch, mixed
   with 1/4 cup water

Take the meat out of the refrigerator to let it come to room temperature (cold meat is tough and takes longer to cook). Preheat the oven to 425°F. Heat a very large, heavy flameproof casserole over a high heat and add the vegetable oil. Working in batches if necessary, brown the meat on its fat side until the surface turns golden and crisp. Turn the meat to its bone side and place the rosemary underneath. Pour in the rice vinegar, mirin, and sake and immediately put the lid on to bring the liquid to a boil. Place the pan in the oven for 12–15 minutes, depending on how well done you like your lamb.

Meanwhile, lightly steam the spinach and warm the beans.

Take the pan out of the oven and remove the meat. Cover it loosely to keep warm. Put the pan over moderate heat to reduce the cooking liquid by a quarter, then add the soy sauce and the cornstarch mixture to thicken. Cut each rack into four portions and serve on a bed of spinach and beans with the sauce poured over it.

tofu and beans

Tofu is one of the oldest processed foods of ancient China and has become a major source of vegetable protein throughout Southeast Asia. The Japanese people first learned of tofu-making in the middle of the sixth century when Buddhism was introduced into Japan. As with many aspects of Chinese culture, the Japanese embraced tofu and refined it to suit the nation's cuisine.

Tofu is made of soya milk and comes in two varieties: the firm cotton variety and the soft silken type. It is rich in high-quality soya protein—4 ounces of tofu contains roughly half the amount of protein of chicken and a third of beef but is much easier to digest. Its oil content consists largely of linoleic acid, which helps to reduce cholesterol levels. Furthermore, tofu contains vitamins B1 and E, and zinc and potassium, which together help to prevent arteriosclerosis, high blood pressure, heart disease, osteoporosis, and diabetes.

I am pleased to see tofu is becoming a healthy alternative to animal protein not only among vegetarians but also among informed health-conscious people. Many organic food shops and Asian food stores sell fresh tofu. Tofu is best kept suspended in a bowl of clean water and refrigerated for up to 3 days. But despite all the good news, both tofu and beans suffer from an image of being rather bland and unsexy. Although both have a mild taste of their own, this makes them highly versatile and accommodating ingredients that can partner many. I hope to show that tofu is not just for Buddhist monks and vegetarians but for everyone.

Five ways of draining tofu Tofu is 90 percent water. Although the water gives it its characteristic softness, some recipes call for drained tofu. Here are five ways of draining it.

Natural way Put a block of tofu on a flat basket lined with a sheet of paper towel and leave it for 2–4 hours.

Poaching method The length of poaching depends on the size of the tofu piece: from 2 minutes for small pieces to 15 minutes for a large whole piece.

Microwave Although this is my least preferred method, it is handy if you are in hurry. Wrap the tofu in paper towels, place it at the center of the turntable and microwave for 3–5 minutes on medium power.

Squeezing method This is a quick and easy method if the shape of the tofu is unimportant. Wrap the tofu in a clean cheesecloth or dishtowel and wring it hard to squeeze out the water.

Pressing This is a good method if you need to retain the tofu's shape but are slightly short on time. Place the tofu on a chopping board, put another chopping board on top and add a weight—a large can of tomatoes is ideal. Depending on the weight, it takes 15–30 minutes to reduce the volume by one third.

Seafood, tofu, and glass noodle salad

This is a refreshing, flavorful salad that involves no cooking.

1 pound firm cotton tofu

2 ounces vermicelli noodles

8 ounces ready-cooked mixed
   seafood

8 cherry tomatoes, halved

generous handful of fresh mint
   and cilantro leaves,
   coarsely chopped

for the salad dressing

1/4 cup Thai fish sauce

1/4 cup lime juice

1 1/2 tablespoons palm sugar
   or brown sugar

1/4 cup water

1 garlic clove, peeled and
   crushed

1/2 large red chile (serrano or
   jalapeño), minced

Use your hands to break the tofu into bite-sized chunks. Let drain in a colander at least 30 minutes.

Meanwhile, soften the noodles: put them in a heat-resistant bowl, cover with boiling water, and let sit for 10–15 minutes. Tear the lettuce into bite-sized pieces.

Drain the noodles and chop them into manageable-sized lengths with a pair of kitchen scissors. In a bowl, mix together all the ingredients for the dressing and set aside.

In a large serving dish, toss all the salad ingredients together. Pour in the salad dressing, toss again, and serve.

Cook's tip

For a vegetarian version, omit the seafood salad and replace the Thai fish sauce with soy sauce.

Tofu cheese

Here are three easy ways to preserve tofu to make it more like cheese. Each recipe makes a wonderful flavored tofu but the texture resembles that of cheese. Eat it on its own as a healthy snack, put it in salads or serve it as tapas with a glass of wine. See page 110 for how to drain tofu.

Miso-flavored tofu

8 ounces medium-colored miso
   of your choice
2 tablespoons mirin
8 ounces firm cotton tofu,
   well drained

Combine the miso and mirin and mix well. Cover the bottom of a glass container with one third of the miso mixture. Place the well-drained tofu in the container and cover it with the rest of the miso. Refrigerate for 3–4 days before eating. The miso mixture can be used once or twice more but reheat it first to get rid of any excess water released by the tofu.

Red wine vinegar pickled tofu

8 ounces soft silken tofu,
   well drained
1–2 garlic cloves, peeled and
   slightly crushed
¹/₄ cup honey
³/₄ cup red wine vinegar

Cut the drained tofu into cubes to fit snugly in a glass jar. Add the garlic. Mix the honey and vinegar well. Gently pour the vinegar mixture into the jar and set aside for 3–5 days to pickle at room temperature.

Spicy chili-flavored tofu

8 ounces firm cotton tofu,
   well drained
1–2 garlic cloves, peeled and
   slightly bruised
1–2 large chiles, sliced lengthwise
   and seeded
1 teaspoon salt
³/₄ cup extra virgin olive oil

Cut the drained tofu into bite-sized pieces. Put them in a glass jar with all the other ingredients. Set aside for 3–5 days at room temperature.

Four tofu dips

Tofu makes a perfect base for dips: it is easy to handle, its mild taste blends with any ingredient or seasoning and, above all, it is very healthy. Here are three quick and easy recipes for party dips with a difference.

Sesame and miso tofu dip

8 ounces tofu of your choice

¼ cup toasted sesame
  seeds

1 tablespoon sugar

2–3 tablespoons medium-
  colored smooth miso paste

1–2 teaspoons soy sauce

Drain the tofu with the squeezing method (see page 110). In a large mortar, grind the sesame seeds until smooth—the resulting paste should resemble smooth peanut butter (which is a perfect substitute for sesame paste). Add the drained tofu and the rest of the ingredients and continue to grind until the mixture is well incorporated and smooth. Adjust the seasoning with more soy sauce if necessary.

Curry tofu dip

8 ounces firm cotton tofu

1 tablespoon curry paste

1 teaspoon soy sauce

1 teaspoon medium-colored
  smooth miso paste

Drain the tofu with the squeezing method (see page 110). Put the tofu and other ingredients in a mortar and grind until the mixture is well blended.

Avocado and onion tofu dip

8 ounces soft silken tofu

1 ripe avocado, peeled and mashed

1 tablespoon lemon juice

1 shallot, chopped

1 teaspoon hot red pepper sauce,
  such as Tabasco (optional)

salt and black pepper

Drain the tofu with the squeezing method (see page 110). Put the tofu, avocado, lemon juice, and shallot in a blender or food processor and blend until the mixture is smooth. Adjust the seasoning with Tabasco, salt and pepper.

Tofu and avocado with wasabi soy dressing

Both silky tofu and buttery avocado have an affinity for punchy wasabi soy dressing. You may keep the recipe as vegetarian or, if you wish, add a few slices of smoked salmon or crispy bacon bits. Either way, this is a healthy, fresh, quick and easy appetizer.

About 1 pound soft silken tofu

1 ripe avocado

1/2 tablespoon lemon juice

1 ripe tomato, sliced

few basil leaves, torn or
shredded

for the wasabi soy dressing

3 tablespoons extra virgin
   olive oil

2 tablespoons soy sauce

2 teaspoons wasabi powder,
   mixed with 2 teaspoons water

1/2 teaspoon sugar or a drop
   of honey

Drain the tofu (see page 110) and refrigerate.

Meanwhile, put all the ingredients for the dressing in a small glass jar with a lid and shake vigorosly to blend.

Cut the chilled tofu into bite-sized pieces. Peel and slice the avocado, discarding the pit, and gently toss in lemon juice to prevent discoloration.

Arrange the tofu, avocado, and tomato on a large serving plate or individual plates. Shake the jar of dressing again and drizzle over the tofu. Garnish with torn or shredded basil leaves and serve.

Tofu, tomato, and mushroom stew

This is a truly comforting dish—guaranteed to warm up the body and soul. Serve it with a loaf of crusty bread to soak up all the juices.

1 pound soft silken tofu

1 tablespoon vegetable oil

1 onion, peeled and
   thickly sliced

2 celery ribs, strings removed
   and coarsely chopped

12 cherry tomatoes, halved

4 ounces mushrooms

3 tablespoons frozen peas

fresh flat-leaf parsley, chopped

for the cooking liquid

1/3 cup water

3 tablespoons white wine

sprigs of oregano and thyme

2 bay leaves

salt and black pepper

To drain the tofu wrap in paper towels and place 2–3 plates on top for 30 minutes. Chop the tofu into bite-sized pieces.

Mix together all the ingredients for the cooking liquid.

Heat a skillet over a moderate heat and add the vegetable oil. Add the onion slices and sauté for 5 minutes or until softened. Add the tofu cubes and brown them lightly. Add the rest of the vegetables and pour in the cooking liquid. Bring it to a boil, then reduce the heat to low and cook for another 10 minutes before turning off the heat. Adjust the seasoning with salt and pepper. Garnish with the parsley and serve.

Cook's tip

Although I call this a stew, it is in fact a very quick dish to prepare. But if you prefer to cook it in the oven, omit all the precooking, put everything in a buttered ovenproof dish and place it in the oven for 20 minutes. I also find a sprinkling of nutmeg really brings out the flavor.

Tofu steak with garlic and mushrooms

Who said tofu is for genteel vegetarians? Tofu has about a third of the amount of protein in beef without the worries of high cholesterol. This is a substantial main-course dish packed with taste and health that could easily out-flavor a beef steak.

Drain the tofu (see page 110). It is a matter of personal choice, but don't overdo as it will leave you with rather solid steaks.

Heat the vegetable oil in a skillet and sauté the garlic slices until they become crisp and the oil is infused. Add the mushrooms and cook until they become soft. Season with soy sauce and adjust the taste with salt and pepper.

Spoon out the mushrooms and their cooking juices and keep them warm. Add more oil if necessary and cook the drained tofu steaks on one side for 5–7 minutes or until they turn crispy golden brown. Cook on the other side. Put the tofu on warmed plates, spoon the mushrooms and garlic slices over the top, garnish with the chopped scallions, and serve immediately.

Cook's tip

Why not serve this with purple-sprouting broccoli with mustard soy dressing (see page 36), grilled asparagus in dashi (page 38), or string beans with sesame miso dressing (page 45)?

4 firm cotton tofu blocks, each
   weighing about 8 ounces
1 tablespoon vegetable oil
2 garlic cloves, peeled and
   thinly sliced
2¹/₂ ounces shimeji mushrooms,
   separated
4 shiitake mushrooms, stems
   discarded and caps sliced
2 tablespoons soy sauce
salt and black pepper
2 scallions, finely chopped

Tofu sashimi with spicy hot oil

This recipe is inspired by both Chinese and Vietnamese cuisine. The only cooking required is to make the garlic- and chile-infused oil.

1 pound soft silken tofu, drained (see page 112) and chilled

2 tablespoons rice grains

2 tablespoons soy sauce

for the spicy oil

1 large red chile (serrano or jalapeño)

¼ cup grapeseed oil or sunflower oil

1 teaspoon Asian sesame oil

2 garlic cloves, peeled and slightly crushed

Cut the drained tofu into bite-sized pieces and arrange on individual serving plates. Refrigerate.

To dry-toast the rice grains, heat the rice in a small nonstick skillet over a high heat, constantly shaking the pan. Grind the toasted rice with a pestle and mortar.

For the spicy oil, cut 2–3 incisions lengthwise on the chile. In a small saucepan, heat the oil, garlic, and chile over a very low heat. Discard the chile and garlic when they turn light brown. Turn the heat to high. Take the plates of tofu out of the fridge, pour over the soy sauce and sprinkle with the ground rice. When the oil is almost smoking, pour it over the tofu and serve immediately.

Warm tofu and steamed vegetable salad with plum dressing

You can make this salad as substantial as you wish by adding steamed vegetables of your choice. You may also add shredded steamed chicken breast.

1 pound soft silken tofu, drained

1 pound spinach

8 ounces bean sprouts, roots
   trimmed

1 medium carrot, peeled
   and cut into matchstick-
   sized pieces

8 fresh shiitake mushrooms,
   stems removed, caps sliced

2 tablespoons vegetable oil

1 teaspoon sesame oil

for the umeboshi dressing

6 tablespoons rice vinegar

4 umeboshi (pickled plums),
   finely mashed

1 tablespoon soy sauce

1 tablespoon sugar

1 garlic clove, peeled and grated

1/2 teaspoon salt

Wrap the tofu with paper towels and let drain for 30 minutes. Bring a saucepan of water to a boil and add the spinach, then immediately turn off the heat and drain the spinach. Squeeze the excess water from it. Steam the rest of the vegetables and cover them to keep warm.

Mix together all the ingredients for the umeboshi dressing and set aside.

Cut the drained tofu into 1/2-inch cubes. Arrange the vegetables and tofu in a large warm serving dish. Put the vegetable oil and sesame oil in a metal cooking spoon and heat until the oil mixture is almost smoking hot. Pour it over the salad and add the dressing. Toss and serve immediately.

Japanese bean ratatouille

This is based on an old bean dish called *gomokumame*—five kinds of beans—that has no fixed list of ingredients but is just a frugal way of using up leftover vegetable with soya beans. Konbu and dried shiitake mushrooms with the soy-based cooking liquid give a homely, comforting taste to the dish. For convenience, I use canned mixed beans that are available from supermarkets.

   Dried beans of any variety need long soaking and cooking. Soak the beans overnight in a large saucepan with four times their volume in water. Rinse the beans and change the water. Cover the beans with enough water and bring to a boil over a high heat, reduce the heat to low/moderate once it reaches a boil and continue to simmer for 45–60 minutes, until the beans are tender.

1 postcard-sized piece of dried
   konbu (kelp seaweed)
2–3 dried shiitake mushrooms
1 cup mixed beans, drained
1 small carrot, peeled and cut
   into small dice
2 tablespoons sugar
¹/₂ teaspoon salt
2 tablespoons soy sauce

With a pair of kitchen scissors, cut the konbu into small postage-stamp-sized pieces and leave them in enough warm water to soften. Reserve the liquid.

Soften the shiitake mushrooms in enough warm water to cover. Drain, reserving the liquid, and chop the caps into similar-sized pieces to the konbu.

Put the drained beans, konbu, mushrooms, and diced carrot in a saucepan with the reserved liquids. Add the sugar and bring to a boil over a moderate heat. Once the mixture reaches a boil, reduce the heat to low and continue to simmer for another 15–20 minutes or until the liquid is almost evaporated. Turn off the heat and adjust the seasoning with salt and soy sauce before serving.

Cook's tip

The bean ratatouille will keep for 2–3 days refrigerated. You can serve it as a small side dish or with salad leaves.

Soya beans with bonito flakes

Soya beans are the favorite and most important beans in Japanese cuisine. There are so many ingredients and seasonings that are made of them—miso paste, soy sauce, and tofu, to name but a few.

¹/₂ tablespoon vegetable oil

²/₃ cup dried soya beans, soaked and drained (see page 122)

1 tablespoon sake

1 tablespoon mirin

1 tablespoon soy sauce

¹/₂ teaspoon hot red chile flakes

¹/₄ ounce bonito flakes

Heat a skillet over a low heat and add the vegetable oil. Add the softened beans and sauté for a few minutes. Add the sake, mirin, and soy sauce and let the cooking liquid reduce by half. Sprinkle with the chili flakes and add the bonito flakes. Toss the beans to mix and serve either hot or at room temperature.

Fava bean "frittata"

I invented this recipe when my children complained that they had simply had enough of our homegrown fava beans. This makes a tasty one-plate lunch or appetizer served with a drizzle of teriyaki sauce (see page 167).

3 pounds fava beans, removed from pods (about 7 ounces)

4 ounces cooked shrimp

1 free-range egg, lightly beaten

2 scallions, finely chopped

2 tablespoons rice flour or cornstarch

1 tablespoon light soy sauce

1 teaspoon peeled and grated fresh ginger

1 tablespoon vegetable oil

Cook the fava beans in a saucepan of boiling water for 10–15 minutes or until they are soft. You should be able to squash a bean between your thumb and index finger. Drain, rinse under cold running water and remove the skins.

Put the beans and shrimp in a blender or food processor and process very briefly—some of the beans and shrimp should be identifiable in shapes. Put the mixture in a bowl, add the egg, scallions, rice flour, soy sauce, and ginger, and mix well.

Heat the oil in a skillet and pour in the egg mixture. Spread it with a spatula to make a flat pancake. Cook on one side for 6–8 minutes over a moderate heat and turn it over to cook the other side for 5 minutes. Serve immediately.

rice and sushi

A third of the world's population depends on rice as its staple diet. Indeed rice is the staple food of Japan, but for the Japanese the real meaning of this humble grain goes far beyond the boundaries of food. Rice and Japanese history, politics, economy, religion, culture, and in fact almost every aspect of the country and its nation's life are inextricably tied together. The labor-intensive and high-maintenance demands of rice cultivation are said to have contributed to forming the industrious and group-cohesive characteristics of the Japanese people. Rice is the soul of Japan and those who understand it hold the key to a real understanding of the country and Japanese cuisine.

Rice plays the central role in Japanese cooking. Whether it is early spring and the very first succulent bamboo shoots are available from Kyoto, or the freshest wild sea bream sashimi from the Shimonoseki Straits, or a thick juicy Kobe beef steak, a humble bowl of cooked rice is the main dish and everything else is an accompanying sideshow. In the Japanese language, the word for cooked rice, *gohan*, is the same as the word for a meal. Millions of Japanese mothers and wives call out, "*Gohan desuyo*" when a meal is ready, because rice and a meal are synonymous.

Nutritionally, rice comprises 75 percent carbohydrate and 8 percent protein, which is the highest protein content of all grains. However, much of the goodness such as edible fiber, vitamins, and minerals are lost in the polishing. In the past, polished white rice was considered the best and was what all Japanese aspired to eat. In my grandmothers' era the loss of those nutrients in rice was easily made up by other food that was not as highly processed as the food we eat today. While unpolished brown rice is harder to digest, it is unquestionably healthier than white rice; it has four times more edible fiber, vitamin B1 and E, twice as much vitamin B2, fat, iron, and phosphorus than polished white rice. After the economic boom of the 1980s followed by over a decade of recession, Japanese people seem to have rediscovered the wisdom of simpler traditional ways of eating that are more suited and kinder to their bodies and souls.

Today Japanese people are eating about half the amount of rice that they used to forty years ago. In 2000, the average annual rice consumption *per capita* fell below 143lbs after peaking at 261lbs in 1962. The irony is that brown rice has become the preferred choice of informed and health-conscious Japanese people, rather than polished white rice which used to be revered as a food for the rich and powerful.

Both my grandmothers believed in the nourishing and healing power of rice, especially when it was cooked in congees—soupy rice. If I sneezed more than three times, I was sure to be given a bowl of steaming hot creamy miso, white spring onion, and ginger congee and swiftly sent to bed. When I had a bad tummy, it was a bowl of tepid warm silky white rice congee with a spoonful of pickled plums. Congees are the ultimate comfort food—easy to make, versatile, and very easy to digest.

Asparagus and fava bean domburi

Domburi, which translates as "on rice," is the Japanese equivalent of a peanut butter and jelly sandwich. It is a quick and easy, satisfying one-bowl snack—almost anything can be turned into a tasty topping sauce served on rice. In this recipe, two spring vegetables are used together.

40 fava beans

4 ounces frozen cooked shrimp

2 asparagus spears

3/4 cup water

2 teaspoons vegetable oil

1 tablespoon light soy sauce

1/2 teaspoon rice vinegar

1 tablespoon cornstarch, mixed
  with 2 tablespoons water

salt and black pepper

2 1/2 cups cooked rice, kept warm

Pod the fava beans to yield 40 individual beans. Boil them for 3 minutes, drain and let them cool before removing the skin from each bean. I know this is fiddly but the end result makes such a difference in taste, color, and texture; it is well worth the extra effort.

Meanwhile put the frozen shrimp in the measured water to defrost and soak. Discard the tough, woody ends of the asparagus spears and slice the rest diagonally.

Heat a wok or skillet over moderate heat and add the oil. Stir-fry both the fava beans and asparagus for 2–3 minutes, then add the prawns and the water. Let the mixture come to a boil and reduce the heat. Season with the soy sauce and vinegar and add the cornstarch mixture to thicken the sauce. Adjust the taste with salt and pepper. Divide the cooked rice among individual bowls, put the asparagus and bean mixture on top, and serve.

Cook's tip

The recipe works equally well if you use crabmeat or any white fish flakes instead of shrimp.

My version of New Year herbal congee

The seventh of January is known as the day of *nanakusa* (seven herbs) and it is the tradition on that day in Japan to prepare and eat seven-herb congee to pray for the good health of the family for the rest of the year. When I was a little girl, I followed my grandmother to nearby fields to forage for those seven wild herbs, such as wild celery, shepherd's purse, wild chrysanthemum, and chickweed, which at that time I thought were more like weeds.

The tradition of preparing the seven-herb congee on the seventh day of January lives on in Japan, perhaps because the herbs (specially grown for the day) can now be bought from supermarkets. Scepticism aside, it does make good sense to treat your body gently with an easily digestible congee after the festive indulgence of Christmas and New Years. I have created my own version of the seven-herb congee with more familiar vegetables and herbs, but have kept the integrity of the original recipe.

1 cup Japanese-style brown rice, rinsed

4 dried shiitake mushrooms

4 cups dashi broth (see pages 16–17) or water

1 medium leek, trimmed and thinly sliced

1 cup purple sprouting (or other thin-stemmed) broccoli, coarsely chopped

1 cup flat-leaf parsley, finely chopped

2 cups spinach, coarsely chopped

2 cups arugula leaves, coarsely chopped

1 cup cilantro leaves, finely chopped

1 heaping tablespoon light-colored miso paste

2 tablespoons light soy sauce

salt

1 tablespoon rice vinegar

1 tablespoon toasted sesame seeds

Rinse the rice until the water runs clear and set it aside in a sieve or colander for at least 1 hour (but preferably 2 hours) before cooking.

In a large heavy saucepan, combine the shiitake mushrooms, broth or water, and the rice. With the lid on, bring the liquid to a boil over a moderate heat and reduce the heat to low once it begins to boil; stir occasionally.

Remove the shiitake mushrooms with a slotted spoon and let them cool before discarding the stems. Thinly slice the caps and put them back into the rice. Add the leek and purple sprouting broccoli, stir and allow to come back to a boil before adding the parsley, spinach, arugula, and cilantro.

Gently stir and return to a boil. Add the miso paste (the taste of the miso should not be prominent, but just give a subtle depth to the broth) and soy sauce. Adjust the seasoning with salt and turn off the heat. Pour in the rice vinegar and stir. Sprinkle with the sesame seeds and serve immediately.

Spicy garlic and chive fried rice

In a Japanese household, there is always some leftover cooked rice and there are numerous ways of making it into tasty dishes. This recipe is one of my summer staples, the other being simple cold noodles. It is very easy and quick to make but, above all, it has a truly appetizing scent and flavor—guaranteed to pick you up when you are feeling a little under the weather in the relentless summer heat.

2 tablespoons vegetable oil

1 teaspoon Asian sesame oil

4 large garlic cloves, peeled and
  minced

2¹/₂ cups cold cooked rice

1 large red chile, seeded and
  finely chopped

2 tablespoons chives, finely
  chopped

1 heaping teaspoon curry powder

2 tablespoons soy sauce

salt and black pepper

2 tablespoons cilantro leaves,
  roughly chopped

Put a wok or large nonstick skillet over a high heat and add the vegetable oil. Reduce the heat to moderate and add the sesame oil and crushed garlic to cook until the oil has become infused and the garlic is golden. Add the rice and, with a spatula, make cut-and-turn "folding" motions to coat the rice with the oil and heat for 3 minutes.

Add the chopped chile and chives and mix, using the cut-and-turn motion. Sprinkle with the curry powder. Drizzle the soy sauce around the edge of the wok and stir. Adjust the taste with salt and pepper and turn the heat off. Garnish with the chopped cilantro leaves and serve immediately.

Leek, hijiki, and tofu miso congee

This is a truly nourishing, tasty and above all comforting dish of soupy flavored rice with miso. Although it is a vegetarian recipe, both tofu and miso supply masses of protein, while hijiki (seaweed) is packed with calcium, iron, and magnesium, not to mention edible fiber. Leeks warm up your body and are known to ward off colds. Altogether this is a perfect winter rice dish to keep your body and soul warm and healthy.

8 ounces firm cotton tofu,
    drained (see page 110)
4 dried shiitake mushrooms
1 postcard-sized piece of konbu
    (dried kelp seaweed)
4 cups water
2 medium leeks, trimmed
    and thinly sliced diagonally
1/4 cup dried hijiki
2 1/2 cups cooked rice
1/4 cup soy sauce
4 ounces medium-colored miso
    paste of your choice

Drain the tofu as described on page 110.

Meanwhile, put the shiitake mushrooms, konbu, and 4 cups water in a heavy saucepan. Put the saucepan on low heat and bring to a boil. Add the sliced leeks, hijiki, and cooked rice and continue to simmer for 15 minutes, stirring occasionally, to thicken.

Cut the drained tofu into bite-sized pieces and add them to the rice mixture. Return to a boil and season with the soy sauce and miso paste. The miso paste needs to be dissolved gradually by adding it with a small amount of liquid or by putting the paste in a sieve and mixing it into the liquid. Bring immediately back to a boil, turn off the heat and serve immediately.

Shimeji mushroom and chicken rice

This is an autumn comfort dish packed with earthy tastes and flavors. By adjusting the amount of liquid, you can make it more like soupy risotto or fluffy pilaf, depending on your mood. This recipe is to make the latter.

1 cup Japanese-style rice
4 chicken tenders (mini chicken breast fillets), sliced diagonally
1 tablespoon sake
1 tablespoon soy sauce
1 package of shimeji mushrooms (about 5 ounces)
few sprigs of cilantro, coarsely chopped
1 lime, cut into 8 wedges

for the cooking liquid
1 cup dashi broth (see pages 16–17)
2 tablespoons sake
2 tablespoons soy sauce
1 tablespoon mirin

Put the rice in a sieve placed inside a bowl. Pour over just enough water to cover and give it three or four firm stirs with your hand. Change the water and do the same again—you will probably have to repeat this stir-and-rinse process two or three more times before the water becomes clear. Drain the rice and set it aside for at least 30 minutes, but preferably 1 hour.

Meanwhile, put the chicken in a bowl with the sake and soy sauce and set aside until the rice is ready to cook. Cut off the base of the shimeji mushrooms where they are joined and separate them.

Put the rice in a heavy saucepan with a tight-fitting lid. Stir in all the ingredients for the cooking liquid. Bring to a boil over a moderate heat. Let it boil for 3 minutes and add the chicken and mushrooms, lower the heat and allow to steam-cook with the lid on for 15 minutes. Turn off the heat and let sit 10 minutes before lifting up the lid to stir. Garnish with the chopped cilantro and serve with lime wedges.

Sushi

A high-ranking Japanese diplomat once told me that the little piece of sushi has probably been more successful in raising Japan's profile on the international stage than all his official efforts. I thought that he was a little too hard on himself but there is a grain of truth in it. Sushi has put Japan on the world culinary map. When I first came to England in the early 1970's, there was only a handful of Japanese restaurants in London; now there are over one hundred in the capital alone and more than half of them serve sushi regularly. Never in my wildest dreams did I think that thirty years later I would see sushi lunch boxes on sale next to sandwiches in supermarkets. Sushi is a perfect portable meal—a fresh, healthy, and good-looking food that is easy to eat anywhere at any time. But sushi is not all about little rice nuggets and slices of raw fish; *nigiri zushi*, the hand-formed sushi, is only one type. It is a relative newcomer in the context of the lengthy evolution of sushi, that began as a way of preserving fish that took as long as a year to make. Sushi has evolved from an ancient slow food to a contemporary fast food with widespread international recognition.

Sushi comes in a wide variety of styles and shapes; each family has its own favorite repertoire and there are countless regional specialities found across Japan. *Chirashi zushi,* or scattered sushi, is a generic term for free-form rice salad that is the easiest to make, highly versatile and very homey. A big dish of scattered sushi always graces the table at family gatherings. The choice of toppings is infinite but I always try to remember the simple principle of choosing seasonal ingredients that work well together in taste, texture, and appearance.

It is impossible to cover the whole spectrum of sushi in one small section of a book when the subject deserves an entire book of its own. I have put together delicious, easy-to-prepare scattered sushi recipes for this section.

How to prepare sushi rice

Good sushi begins with good rice. Try to choose good-quality Japanese-style short-grain rice that you can buy from large supermarkets and Asian stores. The rice is first cooked and seasoned with a sushi vinegar mixture of rice vinegar, salt, and sugar. Once prepared, sushi rice needs to be covered with a clean damp cloth until needed and should be used within the same day. There is no need to refrigerate it as the vinegar has an antibacterial preservative quality; and refrigeration spoils the delicate flavor and hardens the rice. In Japan, every sushi shop has its own sushi vinegar recipe—the general rule is that the stronger the filling or topping served with it, the saltier and less sweet the vinegar mixture. The amount given below is a basic guide and you may vary it.

1¹/₂ cups Japanese-style short-grain rice
1 postcard-sized piece of konbu (dried kelp seaweed)
1¹/₂ cups water

for the sushi vinegar mixture
6 tablespoons rice vinegar
2 tablespoons granulated sugar
1 teaspoon salt

Put the rice in a sieve and submerge it in a large bowl of water. With your hand, keep circling the rice to wash it, then discard the milky water. Keep washing the rice and changing the water until it runs clear. After the final draining, set the rice aside for at least 30 minutes to absorb the moisture clinging to the grains.

Make a few incisions in the konbu to help release its flavor as it cooks. Put the rice, measured water, and konbu in a heavy saucepan with a tight-fitting lid. Bring to a boil over a low/moderate heat. Resist the temptation to lift the lid to take a look while it is cooking. Instead learn to listen for the bubbling sound of boiling. Turn up the heat and cook for another 3–5 minutes, then turn off the heat and let sit 10–15 minutes.

Put the vinegar, sugar, and salt in a non-metallic bowl and stir to dissolve the sugar and salt. Transfer the cooked rice into a moistened (to prevent the rice from sticking), shallow, flat-bottomed dish (an oilfree wooden salad bowl is ideal). Sprinkle a small amount of the sushi vinegar mixture over a spatula into the rice. At the same time, have someone standing by to fan the rice. With a cut-and-turn motion, coat the grains of rice with the vinegar mixture as you separate them. Continue to sprinkle the vinegar into the rice until it looks glossy and has cooled to room temperature. Cover the rice with a clean damp cloth and set aside until needed.

Broccoli and scrambled egg scattered sushi

Try to use purple sprouting or another tender stem broccoli (such as broccolini or broccoli rabe), that I love for their taste and texture.

2 tablespoons butter

2 free-range eggs, lightly beaten

1 tablespoon mirin

pinch of salt

8 ounces broccoli (preferably purple-sprouting or tender stem), trimmed

1 tablespoon rice vinegar

2 cups prepared sushi rice (see page 133)

1 tablespoon sesame seeds

2 tablespoons shredded nori

Put a nonstick skillet over moderate heat and melt the butter. Pour in the beaten eggs with the mirin and use two pairs of chopsticks to scramble the egg mixture into tiny fluffs. When you think you have scrambled enough, turn off the heat and let the egg cool in the pan.

Meanwhile, chop the broccoli diagonally into small pieces and steam. Pour in the rice vinegar into a large, non-metallic bowl and swirl it around to coat the inside—this will stop the rice sticking to the bowl. Add the prepared sushi rice and the steamed broccoli pieces and mix well. Transfer the sushi mixture on to a large serving dish, sprinkle the scrambled eggs and the sesame seeds over the top, garnish with the shredded nori and serve.

Cook's tip

Try this recipe with steamed asparagus in the late spring. I often add salmon flakes (see page 69) to make a one-course meal.

Smoked salmon, salmon roe, and caper sushi

I had to invent this recipe when I was warned at the eleventh hour that one of my dinner-party guests "really does not care for raw fish but loves sushi."

2 tablespoons rice vinegar

2 cups prepared sushi rice
  (see page 133)

juice of 1 lime

8 ounces smoked salmon
  (offcuts are fine)

3 tablespoons capers, drained

1 tablespoon sake

1 jar of salmon roe (about 1 ounce)

Moisten the inside of a large mixing bowl with the rice vinegar to stop the rice from sticking. Put in the prepared sushi rice and pour in the lime juice to help loosen the rice. Add the smoked salmon bits and capers and mix with a flat spatula using a cut-and-turn motion. Add the sake to the salmon roe—this helps to take away its fishy smell and makes the roe less sticky. Transfer the sushi mixture on to a large serving platter, scatter the salmon roe on top and serve.

Cook's tip

If you find it difficult to get salmon roe (normally sold in small glass jars), try finely scrambled eggs instead.

Marinated tuna, avocado, and white onion sushi

This recipe shows a great partnership between Japanese and Western ingredients.

8 ounces sashimi-quality tuna

1 small white onion

1 ripe avocado

1 tablespoon rice vinegar

2 cups prepared sushi rice
  (see page 133)

2 tablespoons wasabi powder,
  mixed with 2 tablespoons water

1 sheet of dried nori, finely shredded

for the marinade

3 tablespoons soy sauce

3 tablespoons toasted sesame seeds

1 tablespoon mirin

2 teaspoons wasabi powder,
  mixed with 1/4 cup water

Cut the tuna into 1/4 inch-thick slices. Mix together all the marinade ingredients and marinate the tuna for 15–20 minutes.

Meanwhile, thinly slice the white onion and put in a bowl of ice-cold water—soaking gets rid of the onion's smell and freshens it up. Peel the avocado, slice it into similar-sized pieces as the tuna and sprinkle with the rice vinegar to prevent discoloring.

Divide the prepared sushi rice into four and put into individual serving dishes. Place the avocado pieces over the sushi rice and arrange the marinated tuna on top. Drain the onion slices and divide into four portions to scatter on top of the tuna. Place a small mound of wasabi paste on the center, garnish with shredded nori and serve.

Shrimp, pomegranate, and green chile sushi

Pomegranates originated in the Middle East and are widespread throughout Asia. They were brought to Japan from China in the twelfth century; the flowers were used for ornamental and the fruits for medicinal purposes. There are many references to them in medieval Japanese paintings and literature.

2 ripe pomegranates

¼ cup pomegranate juice

2 cups prepared sushi rice (see page 133)

8 ounces cooked shrimp

1–2 large green chiles, finely chopped

few sprigs of cilantro and mint leaves

Halve the pomegranates horizontally and separate the individual seeds from the rind and reserve. Moisten the inside of a large mixing bowl with 2 tablespoons of the pomegranate juice to stop the rice sticking. Add the prepared sushi rice, sprinkle over the remainder of the pomegranate juice to separate the rice and mix. Add the cooked shrimp, chopped chiles, and reserved pomegranate and mix with a flat spatula in a cut-and-turn motion. Transfer the sushi mixture into either a large serving dish or individual dishes. Garnish with the cilantro and mint leaves and serve.

Cook's tip

This recipe works equally well with crabmeat instead of shrimp.

Chicken teriyaki and edamame sushi salad

Here is a recipe for meat-eating sushi lovers. An unusual combination of chicken and sushi rice works well, with edamame as an additional bonus.

12 ounces boneless, skinless
  chicken thighs
2 tablespoons cornstarch
1 tablespoon vegetable oil
1/3 cup teriyaki sauce
  (see page 167)
1 cup frozen edamame
a little rice vinegar (optional)
2 cups prepared sushi rice
  (see page 133)
1 sheet of dried nori, torn into
  small pieces

Cut the chicken thighs into bite-sized pieces and dust them with the cornstarch. Heat a nonstick skillet over moderate heat and add the vegetable oil. Sauté the chicken for 5 minutes or until golden. Add the teriyaki sauce and bring to a boil, then reduce the heat to low to simmer until the liquid has almost evaporated.

Meanwhile, either steam or boil the edamame for about 3 minutes. Remove them from their pods, if needed, and set them aside.

Moisten the inside of a large mixing bowl with either water or, better yet, rice vinegar to stop the rice from sticking. Add the prepared sushi rice and the chicken and mix with a flat spatula in a cut-and-turn motion. Transfer the sushi mixture on to a large serving dish, scatter the edamame on top, garnish with the nori pieces, and serve.

Cook's tip

If you find it difficult to get edamame try using frozen baby fava or lima beans instead. You can prepare this in advance—up to 3 hours beforehand—but do not garnish with the nori until just before serving or it will become limp.

noodles

Like so many things, the noodle-making technique originally came to Japan from China over a thousand years ago. Noodles have become native in Japan and have developed their own national identity. Japanese noodles are broadly divided into two groups by their ingredients—wheat and buckwheat. Wheat-based udon and somen noodles are more popular in the warmer and more fertile south-western part of Japan, while soba noodles, made of buckwheat, are a preferred choice in the colder and harsher north-eastern regions. Indeed, in 722 AD, soba was planted as an emergency supplementary grain when the rice crop failed—it is a perfect follow-on crop after rice as it takes just 75 days from sowing to harvesting.

Noodles are among the most popular foods in Japan. They are eaten everywhere at any time of the day—as a breakfast substitute at a busy railway station, quick lunch in Tokyo's business district or a late-night snack after drinking in the Roppongi entertainment area. They are quick and simple to prepare, instantly satisfying and easy to digest. Noodles contain carbohydrate, protein, vitamins, and minerals. They have very little flavor of their own, so they are an ideal ingredient to cook with others. I hope to demonstrate that Japanese noodles make tasty, easy-to-prepare and above all, comforting and nourishing dishes.

All the recipes in this chapter are designed to serve 2.

How to make noodle dipping sauce

This is a versatile sauce that can be made in advance in a large quantity. The sauce will keep for 2–3 weeks in the fridge in a glass jar. Provided you have used good-quality konbu, shiitake mushrooms and bonito flakes, there is enough flavor left in these ingredients after making the dipping sauce to give taste to another dish: I make a condiment that is delicious and healthy accompaniment for plain boiled rice. Thinly slice the konbu and shiitake mushrooms and put them in a saucepan with ¾ cup water, 1 tablespoon soy sauce and ½ tablespoon mirin. Cook over a gentle heat until nearly all the water has evaporated. Repeat this process three times to intensify the flavor. You should end up with a dark shiny mixture of seaweed and mushrooms. It keeps for up to 1 month in an airtight container in the refridgerator.

2 postcard-sized pieces of konbu
  (kelp seaweed)
4 dried shiitake mushrooms
4³/₄ cups water
³/₄ cup mirin
¹/₃ cup sake
¹/₃ cup soy sauce
1¹/₂ teaspoons sea salt
1¹/₄ ounces bonito flakes

In a large glass bowl, put the konbu and mushrooms in the 4³/₄ cups water and leave to infuse in the refrigerator overnight.

Put the mirin and sake in a large saucepan and bring to a boil over a high heat. Reduce the heat and cook for 2–3 minutes to burn off the alcohol. Add the soy sauce and return to a boil over a high heat. Add the fish flakes once the liquid reaches the boil, then reduce the heat and continue simmering 5 minutes.

Let the sauce cool to room temperature before straining it through a sieve lined with paper towels. Put the sauce in a sterilized glass jar and store in the fridge.

Mushroom soba in broth

In cold weather, it is truly comforting to eat a bowl of hot noodles. It is instantly satisfying and warms you up from inside. Japanese mushrooms such as shiitake, shimeji, and enoki have become increasingly easy to buy in the West. Mushrooms have many beneficial health properties—they lower blood pressure, reduce cholesterol, are anticarcinogenic, and high in fiber.

7 or 8 ounces dried soba noodles

⅓ cup noodle dipping sauce
  (see page 140)

3 cups water

1 pound assorted mushrooms
  of your choice, cleaned and
  sliced

4 scallions, thinly sliced
  diagonally

2 tablespoons toasted sesame
  seeds, coarsely ground

shichimi togarashi (Japanese
  seven-spice seasoning)

serves 2

Bring a large saucepan of water to a boil over a high heat. Add the soba noodles and give a quick stir to ensure the noodle strands are separated. Let the water return to a boil and reduce the heat to moderate.

When the water is about to boil over, add a glass of cold water and let it boil again—this is to ensure both the outer and central parts of the noodle strands are cooked at the same speed. When the water returns to a boil for the third time, drain the noodles and rinse them under cold running water. Drain well and set aside.

In a saucepan, heat the noodle dipping sauce and 3 cups water to make a broth. You may vary the amount of water to suit your taste.

When the broth reaches the boil, briefly submerge the noodles to reheat. (You may do this by placing the noodles in a sieve and lowering into the boiling broth.) Divide the warm noodles between two warmed bowls.

Add the mushrooms to the broth and cook for 2–3 minutes. Ladle the broth over the noodles and add the chopped scallions and sesame seeds. Serve with the shichimi togarashi offered separately.

Soba noodle salad with smoked salmon, salmon roe, and grated daikon

Refreshing grated daikon (Japanese white radish) works as a bridge between the oily smoked salmon and the soba noodles. I recommend using green tea soba noodles for this recipe—it looks prettier. Dried soba noodles often come in bundles tied together with a thin paper ribbon. Each bundle is one serving, if you are hungry.

7 ounces dried soba noodles
(preferably green tea variety)

1 pound daikon (Japanese white
radish)

4 tablespoons salmon roe
(from a jar)

1 tablespoon sake

1/2 white onion, thinly sliced and
soaked in water

1/3 cup noodle dipping sauce
(see page 144)

3–4 ounces smoked salmon,
roughly torn

4 teaspoons wasabi powder,
mixed with 2 teaspoons water

serves 2

Cook the noodles as described on page 141.

Meanwhile, grate the daikon and reserve both the juice and the grated daikon. Put the salmon roe in a small bowl and pour over the sake—this will take the fishy smell away and separate the roe. Drain the sliced white onion.

Mix the reserved juice of the grated daikon with the dipping sauce—you may vary the amount of the dipping sauce to suit your taste. Divide the noodles between two shallow bowls. Arrange the grated daikon, torn smoked salmon pieces, onion slices, and salmon roe on top of the noodles. Put a small mound of wasabi paste on top, pour the dipping sauce over the mixture and serve.

Cook's tip

Try adding some watercress as a garnish—it works wonders.

Sobagetti with crispy bacon and spinach

A number of my friends have given up eating wheat for various reasons. Soba noodles are made of buckwheat flour, which is gluten-free and provides a healthy and tasty alternative to pasta.

7 ounces dried soba noodles

¼ cup olive oil

4–6 thick slices of bacon,
    chopped

1 garlic clove, peeled and crushed

1 cup spinach, coarsely chopped

¼ cup soy sauce

salt and black pepper

serves 2

Cook the soba noodles as described on page 141. Heat a large skillet and add the olive oil and sauté the bacon bits until they become crispy. Reduce the heat to low and cook the garlic for 2–3 minutes before adding the spinach. When the spinach is wilted, add the soy sauce and adjust the seasoning with salt and pepper. Turn off the heat, add the noodles and toss gently. Divide the noodle mixture into two pasta dishes and serve.

Cook's tip

You can use any green vegetables such as broccoli or arugula leaves. It will give added interest if you use Japanese greens such as mizuna, mibuna, or shungiku, which are becoming increasingly popular.

Hijiki pasta

Hijiki, like many other types of seaweed, is very healthy. It is particularly rich in calcium, magnesium, and iron. It is cooked in various forms and is especially popular among middle-aged women for its effectiveness against osteoporosis. It is also believed to have a calming effect and promote a good night's sleep.

¼ cup dried hijiki

14–16 ounces dried udon noodles

¼ cup olive oil

3 garlic cloves, peeled and
    crushed

1 large red chile, seeded
    and finely chopped

6 anchovy fillets, mashed

salt and black pepper

serves 2

Soak the dried hijiki in plenty of water for 15 minutes and drain well. Bring a large saucepan of water to a boil and add the noodles. When the water returns to a boil and begins to boil over, add a cup of cold water. Let the water return to a boil for the third time and take it off the heat, rinse the noodles under cold running water. Drain well and set aside.

Heat a skillet over a moderate heat and add the olive oil, then add the garlic and fry until the oil is infused. Add the hijiki, chopped chile, and anchovies. Add the noodles and toss well. Adjust the seasoning with salt and pepper and serve.

Udon salad with sweet vinegar miso dressing

I often use noodles instead of potatoes for salads. Although udon noodles are used for this recipe, you may experiment with your favorite noodle.

7 ounces dried udon noodles

2 free-range eggs

4–6 lettuce leaves of your choice

1/2 cucumber

1 medium carrot

3–4 small vine-ripened
  tomatoes, halved

for the salad dressing

2 tablespoons toasted sesame
  seeds

4 tablespoons sweet vinegar
  miso (see page 169)

1 tablespoon noodle dipping
  sauce (see page 140)

2–3 tablespoons water

serves 2

Cook the noodles as described on page 146.

Meanwhile, hard-boil the eggs, shell and slice them.

For the dressing, grind the sesame seeds with a pestle and mortar until they become a coarse paste. Add the rest of the dressing ingredients and mix well.

Tear the salad leaves into manageable-sized pieces. Halve the cucumber and carrot lengthwise and slice diagonally.

Place the noodles on a large serving platter and add the salad leaves. Arrange the cucumber, carrot, sliced hard-boiled eggs, and tomatoes on top. Drizzle with the salad dressing and serve.

Beef and leek udon noodle soup

This is a wholesome gutsy noodle soup guaranteed to warm up the body and soul in the cold winter months. Because the authentic recipe calls for scallions with a long white stalk (that is available only from Japanese groceries). I have used leeks instead. Scallions and leeks share similar health properties of warming the body. I often make this dish when I feel that I'm coming down with a cold.

7 ounces dried udon noodles

1 tablespoon vegetable oil

6 ounces beef top round,
  thinly sliced

1 medium leek, thinly sliced
  diagonally

1 thumb-sized piece of fresh
  ginger root, peeled and cut
  into matchstick-sized pieces

1/3 cup noodle dipping sauce
  (see page 140)

2 1/2 cups water

2 tablespoons medium-colored
  miso paste

sansho pepper

serves 2

Cook the noodles in a large saucepan of boiling water for 2–3 minutes. Add a glass of cold water when it is about to boil over. Let the water return to a boil and cook for a further 2–3 minutes. Rinse thoroughly under cold running water and drain well.

Put a saucepan over a moderate heat, add the vegetable oil and sauté the beef and leek. Add the ginger, dipping sauce, and water—you may vary the amount of water to suit your taste. Add the miso paste gradually to ensure it dissolves completely. Add the noodles and continue to heat for another 2–3 minutes, but do not let the liquid boil as this will spoil the miso flavor. Divide the noodle soup between two serving bowls and offer with sansho pepper.

Cook's tip

I will let you into a secret about how to stop meat from sticking to the bottom of a pan. Heat the pan and oil in the usual way and then cool the bottm of the pan by wiping it with a cold damp cloth, taking care not to burn your hand.

Chilled tomato somen

This recipe was born when we were staying in a farmhouse in Umbria in Italy. The old gardener, with a weather-beaten face like a well-worn shoe, spoke no English and my Italian was equally limited. But when he gave me a handful of odd-shaped ripe tomatoes from the garden so I decided to put them together with somen noodles I had brought with us and it was delicious.

1 pound very ripe vine-ripened
  tomatoes
1 garlic clove, peeled and grated
1/2 teaspoon salt
1 1/2 tablespoons soy sauce
3–4 tablespoons extra virgin
  olive oil
7 ounces dried somen noodles
plenty of freshly ground black
  pepper
fresh basil and flat-leaf parsley,
  cut into thin strips

serves 2

Blanch the tomatoes in boiling water and immediately plunge them into ice water. Peel, halve and discard the seeds. Chop them coarsely and mix with the grated garlic, salt, soy sauce, and olive oil. Refrigerate the tomato sauce while you cook the somen noodles. Bring a saucepan of water to a boil and add the noodles. Stir to ensure that the noodles stay separate. Add a glass of cold water when the water is about to boil over. Return to a boil, drain and rinse under cold running water. In a large mixing bowl toss the noodles with the tomato sauce. Divide the noodles between two serving plates, season with pepper, garnish with the fresh herbs and serve.

hotpots

The Japanese have such a fondness for *Nabe ryo¯ri*, the table-top hotpot cooking style for which every region, prefecture and even family has its own favorite recipe. Hotpots are particularly popular during the cold months for birthday celebrations, family gatherings, school reunions, and office parties. Like fondues, hotpots are for fun and sociable occasions when everyone joins in and cooking is simple and done at the table. In Japanese there is a term *nabe bugyo¯*, or 'hotpot sheriff', which describes a person who takes charge of the cooking—it is an affectionate term for husbands and fathers who don't normally enter the kitchen but regard themselves as handy cooks.

It was hard to choose just four recipes for this section since there are literally hundreds but the ones I have selected are all easy to follow and versatile. I recommend that you start with these recipes and, once you feel confident enough, adjust them to suit your own taste and preference.

Four basic rules for a "hotpot sheriff"

1 Keep it simple. Decide on a main ingredient, be it vegetables, meat, chicken, or seafood. It is tempting to put all your favorites in together, but the tastes of a hotpot easily become blurred and confused.

2 Do not skimp on preparation. The simplicity of the actual cooking means the preparation of the ingredients will really affect the final result. Not only is the preparation important for taste, but it also makes the dish more appetizing to look at and easier to eat.

3 Waste not, want not. The soup left at the end is full of flavor—do not waste it, but use it to make another course by adding some cooked rice or noodles to round off a sumptuous meal.

4 Always have larger quantities of the raw ingredients than you think you will need. I am amazed and delighted by the sudden increase in people's appetite when they can participate in cooking for and serving themselves.

Salmon hotpot

This hotpot originates in the Ishikari region of the northern island of Hokkaido. Hokkaido is a cross between the Scottish Highlands and the Wild West. Its barren rugged landscape resembles some parts of the Scottish Highlands and the Ishikari region is particularly famous for its wild salmon. During the nineteenth century, the government encouraged farmers and miners to move north to open up the frontier and even today the islanders retain an adventurous pioneering spirit and see themselves as separate from the rest of the country. This is a gutsy, wholesome hotpot guaranteed to warm up your body and soul.

1¹/₂ pounds salmon fillet

2 tablespoons sake

8 ounces waxy potatoes, cleaned

2 medium carrots, peeled

1 ear corn on the cob

1 pound Chinese cabbage

2 medium leeks, trimmed

4 shiitake mushrooms, stems
  removed

2 tablespoons butter

for the seasoning sauce

4 cups dashi broth
  (see pages 16–17)

3 ounces medium-colored miso
  paste

2 tablespoons soy sauce

2 tablespoons sake

2 tablespoons mirin

Preparation Cut the salmon fillet into bite-sized pieces, pour the sake over the top and set aside.

Steam or boil the potatoes in their skins and cut them into bite-sized pieces. Cut the carrots into big chunks. Cut the ear of corn crosswise into four equal pieces. Cut the cabbage into bite-sized pieces. Cut the leeks diagonally into chunky pieces. Arrange all the vegetables on a large platter.

In a large jar, mix together all the ingredients for the seasoning sauce and stir well to ensure the miso paste is dissolved.

At the table Put a cooking pot on a portable burner in the center of the table. Put all the seasoning sauce in the pot and bring to a boil over a high heat. Add all the other ingredients to the pot when the sauce begins to boil, reduce the heat and let it simmer for 10–15 minutes or until the potatoes are soft. Add the butter and invite the guests to help themselves.

Zen tofu hotpot

I first had this dish at a Zen temple in Kyoto on a chilly autumn day. Although I was only ten years old, the purity and warm sensation of the tofu has remained with me ever since. The authentic recipe calls for the highest-quality tofu that is, sadly, not available outside Japan—so I have added shimeji mushrooms for a bit of extra taste.

for the konbu broth

1 approximately 12-inch square
   piece of konbu (kelp seaweed)
1 pound firm cotten tofu
4 ounces shimeji mushrooms

for the dipping sauce

2 scallions, finely chopped
1/3 cup soy sauce
1/3 cup water
1 1/2 tablespoons mirin
1oz bonito flakes
zest of 1/2 lemon
2 teaspoons crushed hot red
   chile flakes (optional)

Preparation For the konbu stock, soak the konbu in 6 cups water overnight to infuse the konbu's umami (the fifth element of taste).

With a pair of chopsticks, cut the tofu into bite-sized cubes—the reason for using the chopsticks instead of a knife is to leave rough edges so that the sauce has more tofu surface to cling to. Separate the shimeji mushrooms. Arrange the tofu and mushrooms on a large platter.

Combine all the ingredients for the dipping sauce in a saucepan. Bring to a boil over a moderate heat and strain out the solids.

At the table Place a portable burner in the center of the table and put a cooking pot on top. Each guest should have a bowl of dipping sauce. Fill the cooking pot halfway with the prepared konbu broth and turn on the heat. When the broth begins to boil, add the remaining tofu and mushrooms. Reduce the heat to low to simmer for 5 minutes or so, then invite the guests to help themselves. Replenish the pot with tofu and mushrooms as they are eaten.

Hotpot sheriff's tip

If you have a small heat-resistant jug, fill it with the dipping sauce and place it in the center of the cooking pot. This will keep the dipping sauce warm.

Vegetarian hotpot

This is a simple yet tasty vegetarian dish. There are no strict rules as to what you can put in—but try to balance the tastes, textures, and colors. Think of this as a warm vegetable salad. I am also suggesting three varieties of dipping sauce to enjoy.

4 deep-fried tofu blocks

konbu broth (see page 152)

1 pound daikon (Japanese white radish), peeled

1 carrot, peeled

2 medium rutabaga, peeled and cut into bite-sized pieces

for the hot chile soy dipping sauce

1/3 cup sake

3/4 cup soy sauce

3 large red chiles (serrano or jalapeño)

3 large green chiles

1/2 lemon

sesame and sweet miso dipping sauce

1/4 cup toasted sesame seeds

1/4 cup sweet vinegar miso dressing (see page 169)

1/4 cup noodle dipping sauce (see page 140)

100ml water

citrus soy dipping sauce (see page 154)

Preparation Blanch the deep-fried tofu in a saucepan of boiling water for 1 minute to remove any excess oil. Cut the daikon and carrot diagonally into bite-sized pieces. Arrange all the vegetables with the tofu on a large platter.

For the hot chili soy dipping sauce, boil the sake in a saucepan to burn off the alcohol and add the soy sauce. Allow it to return to a boil, then let cool to room temperature. Meanwhile, make incisions lengthwise in the chiles and slice the lemon. Put them in a sterilized jar and pour the soy mixture over them when they have cooled down. Refrigerate and use within 4 weeks.

For the sesame and sweet miso dipping sauce, grind the sesame seeds with a pestle and mortar until smooth. Add the rest of the ingredients and grind to incorporate.

At the table Place a cooking pot on a portable burner in the center of the table. Fill the pot with the konbu broth and add about half of the ingredients. Bring to a boil over a high heat. Reduce the heat to low and offer the hotpot with the three varieties of dipping sauce. Replenish the vegetables as required.

Chicken hotpot

Slow simmering brings out all the goodness and flavor of chicken—make sure you use the best-quality organic birds for this dish. I recommend citrus-flavored soy sauce for dipping—and why not add some cooked rice and beaten eggs to the wonderful cooking juices left at the end to make a comforting rice porridge?

Preparation For the chicken broth, put the chicken carcass in a large saucepan with the dashi broth and sake and bring to a boil over a high heat. Reduce the heat and continue to simmer for another 30 minutes, skimming off any scum that floats to the surface. Remove the chicken and strain the broth; set the broth aside until the cooking starts.

Blanch the chicken thighs in a saucepan of boiling water for 5 minutes, drain and rinse in cold water. Chop the Chinese cabbage into bite-sized pieces. Chop the leeks and carrots diagonally. Separate the shimeji mushrooms. Arrange the vegetables on a large platter.

For the citrus soy dipping sauce, mix together all the ingredients.

At the table Place a portable burner in the center of the table with a cooking pot on top. Each guest should have a bowl of dipping sauce. Fill the cooking pot halfway with the prepared broth and bring it to a boil over a high heat. Put in about a third of the prepared chicken thighs and let the broth return to a boil before adding one third of the vegetables. Reduce the heat to low and simmer for 10–15 minutes, until the vegetables are soft, then invite the guests to help themselves. Replenish the broth, chicken, and vegetables as needed.

1¼ pounds chicken thighs
  on the bone
1 pound Chinese cabbage
1–2 medium leeks, trimmed
1–2 medium carrots, peeled
4 ounces shimeji or oyster
  mushrooms

for the chicken broth
1 chicken carcass, rinsed
8 cups dashi broth
  (see pages 16–17)
⅓ cup sake

**for the citrus soy
dipping sauce**
⅓ cup grapefruit juice
⅓ cup yuzu juice (available in
  bottles from Japanese stores)
  or lime juice
⅓ cup soy sauce

desserts

When I first came to England it took me a while to appreciate the significance of dessert that is nearly always sweet or chocolate-flavored and served at the end of a meal. In the context of a Western-style meal, dessert occupies as important a position as an appetizer or main course. In contrast, a traditional Japanese meal ends with a bowl of rice, miso soup and pickles. A few slices of seasonal fruits described as *mizu gashi* (literally "water sweets") are often served after the rice and soup, but this is not considered a part of the meal.

Yet the Japanese are fond of confectionary of all kinds. They distinguish between *yogashi* (Western-style confectionary) and *wagashi* (Japanese-style). A typical indigenous confection is made from fruits, root vegetables, beans, nuts, seeds, seaweeds, and rice products and never uses any dairy products. These traditional confections are typically consumed either at tea ceremonies or as *oyatsu*—meaning "honorable eight"—it is eaten as a mid-afternoon snack at the

eighth hour on the traditional Japanese clock system—the equivalent of two o'clock in the afternoon. The relatively recent origin of *oyatsu* dates back only to the seventeenth century. Today, as cross-cultural influences become ever more prominent, serving dessert to round off a meal, Japanese or non-Japanese, has become an established custom. In addition, the practice of taking a mid-afternoon snack with tea lives on in Japan in harmony with the adopted Western tradition of serving dessert at the end of the meal.

Choosing dessert recipes for this book proved more challenging than any other chapter because the notion of dessert and the role played by candy is so different in our two cultures. I have tried and, I hope, succeeded in accommodating the expectations of Western diners by selecting recipes that will provide a sense of a treat to round off a meal while preserving the integrity of the traditional Japanese confection.

Dorayaki—pancake with sweet adzuki bean paste

This is so named because in appearance it resembles a *dorayaki*, or copper gong used in Buddhist ceremonies and court music. Provided you have a good supply of homemade sweet adzuki bean paste on hand, it is very easy and quick to make.

1 medium free-range egg
  and 1 egg yolk
$1/3$ cup superfine sugar
1 teaspoon honey
$1/2$ teaspoon baking soda
$2^1/2$ tablespoons water
1 cup all-purpose flour
1 tablespoon vegetable oil
6oz sweet adzuki bean paste
  (see pages 158–159)

**makes approximately
12 pancakes**

In a bowl, lightly beat together the egg and egg yolk. Sift in the superfine sugar. Continue to beat the egg mixture until it turns pale yellow. Add the honey and mix well.

In a separate bowl, dissolve the baking soda in half of the water. Add to the egg mixture. Holding the sieve above the egg mixture, sift in the flour and, with a cut-and-turn motion, fold the flour into the egg mixture. Do not overmix. Cover the bowl with plastic wrap and refrigerate for 20–30 minutes.

Heat a nonstick skillet over moderate heat and add the oil. With a tablespoon, pour in the mixture to make a 3-inch-wide pancake. When small air bubbles begin to appear, flip it over to cook the other side. Repeat the process to make eleven more pancakes of a similar size. Transfer them to a rack to cool.

Divide the adzuki paste into six equal portions. Spread the paste on half of the pancakes and top each with a second pancake to form a sandwich. Eat within 3 days.

Adzuki bean paste

Adzuki bean paste is the most important ingredient used in making *wagashi*—traditional Japanese confections. It is comfortingly sweet but has all the nutritious goodness of adzuki beans including iron, potassium, and edible fiber. These beans are most valuable nutritionally for their antioxidant properties that prevent high blood pressure and other lifestyle-related diseases, as well as cancer. Although readymade varieties are available in cans, homemade adzuki bean paste is always better and it is not difficult to prepare, just time consuming. So I suggest you cook a large amount when you have some spare time and keep it refrigerated.

There are two types of paste, grainy and smooth. The recipe is mostly the same until the beans are blended in a food processor or blender. Smooth adzuki bean paste is like a soft silken tofu in contrast to the more robust firm cotton tofu. It is delectably silky, delicate, and subtly sweet. Refrigerate both pastes in an airtight container and use within three weeks or, alternatively, freeze in small batches.

For the grainy variety

11–12 ounces dried adzuki beans
1/2 cup granulated sugar
pinch of salt

makes approximately
  1 1/3 pounds

Put the beans in a sieve, discard any imperfect ones and rinse under cold running water—handle them gently. Place the beans in a heavy saucepan, add 2 1/2 cups water and bring to a boil over a moderate heat. Add another 3/4 cup cold water to reduce the temperature to soften the beans. Let it return to a boil and simmer for 2 minutes before turning off the heat. Drain and rinse under cold running water. Clean the saucepan and return the beans with 3 1/4 cups water; bring to a boil again over a moderate heat. Keep adding more water to maintain the water temperature just below the boiling point, and continue to simmer for 10 minutes or until the wrinkles on the beans disappear. Drain the beans in a sieve and rinse under cold running water.

Clean the saucepan again and return the beans with 3 1/2 cups water. Put the saucepan over a moderate/high heat and bring to a boil. Lower the heat to simmer for 45–60 minutes. Try to maintain the simmering temperature by adding water from time to time—do not stir at all as it will make the beans tough. Take a spoonful of beans to test their softness. If you can smash them between your fingers without too much effort they are done. Transfer the beans into a sieve and put them in a bowl with some of the cooking liquid. Blend the mixture in a food processor, in 2–3 batches, and give each batch 10–20 seconds of processing. The paste should have a grainy texture with many of the beans still recognizable.

Put half of the bean paste in a large saucepan with the sugar and heat rapidly over a high heat, stirring with a wooden spoon until the liquid starts to boil. Reduce the heat to moderate/low, add the rest of the bean paste and continue to stir, taking care not to let it burn at the bottom, until most of the liquid has evaporated. Add the salt and stir well. Turn off the heat and spread the paste on a large plate or tray to cool. Refrigerate once it has reached room temperature

For the smooth variety

Process the beans until you have a smooth paste. Place a fine sieve over a large bowl and, with plenty of water, wash off the skins of the beans in small batches. Discard the skins, add more water to fill the bowl and stir gently. Let stand for a few minutes to let the mixture settle. By gently tilting the bowl, drain off the cloudy top layer. Repeat this blanching process until the water becomes clear. This is important as it determines the taste of the final bean paste.

Place a clean piece of cheesecloth or dishtowel in a sieve fitted over a bowl. Gently pour in the bean mixture to drain the water. You should be left with a dry, smooth bean mash. Put 5 tablespoons water and the sugar in a saucepan and heat until all the sugar has dissolved. Add half of the bean mash and bring it to a boil over moderate to high heat, stirring all the time to avoid burning—add more water if it is too dry. The consistency you want is not dissimilar to that of cream cheese. The continuous stirring is important as it makes the paste creamier and elastic. When the paste has achieved the desired consistency, spread it on a tray and let cool.

Green tea ice cream and adzuki paste

This is one of my darkest secret short-cut recipes. As there is no tradition of desserts to round off a meal in Japan, I used to, and still do to some extent, find it difficult and often run out of time to prepare a good dessert when I am giving a dinner party. This is my trump card—it is the easiest recipe in this entire book and is a downright cheat with a satisfyingly good result. You need a high-quality vanilla ice cream.

1 pint very good-quality vanilla ice cream of your choice

2 teaspoons matcha (green tea) powder

1 teaspoon lukewarm water

¼ cup homemade sweet adzuki bean paste (see pages 158–159)

Start with softening the ice cream by taking it out of the freezer and transferring it to the fridge for 15–20 minutes—but do not let it melt.

Put the matcha powder in a small, fine-meshed sieve or a tea strainer held over a mixing bowl and push it through. Use the back of a teaspoon to ensure all the tea powder is used. Gently add the water and mix well.

Add half of the ice cream and mix thoroughly with a rubber spatula. Then add the rest of the ice cream. You can stop mixing when the ice cream looks marbled, or you may continue mixing to achieve a uniform pale-green-colored ice cream. Place the bowl in the freezer for 1 to 2 hours, or until the ice cream is firm.

This amount makes eight scoops. Serve each topped with ½ tablespoon of the adzuki bean paste.

Cook's tip

You can make another Japanese-inspired ice cream by simply omitting the tea powder and mixing the sweet adzuki bean paste (see pages 158–159) into the vanilla ice cream.

Seasonal fruit "jewelry box"

You may vary the choice of fruits in this recipe to suit your taste and to take advantage of what is seasonally available. Try to use a variety of appealing colors so the fruits captured in the gelatin resemble shimmering jewels.

1/2 honeydew melon, peeled, seeded, and cut into cubes

8 ounces watermelon, rind removed, seeded, and cut into small cubes

2 Japanese medlars, peeled, pitted, and cut into small cubes (or substitute an orange-colored fruit such as papaya)

1 peach or nectarine, peeled, pitted, and cubed

8 seedless green grapes

8 seedless red grapes

12 blueberries

1/4 cup mirin

2 tablespoons yuzu juice or lime juice

2 1/2 cups water

1/4 cup granulated sugar

2 teaspoons gelatin, soaked in 1 tablespoon cold water

Combine all the fruits in a mixing bowl. Pour in the mirin and yuzu or lime juice and toss gently to coat the fruits with the liquid.

Select four small bowls or coffee cups. Cut four small squares of plastic wrap and use to line the bowls to create molds. Divide the fruit mixture evenly between them.

Heat the 2 1/2 cups water, the sugar, and gelatin in a saucepan over a moderate heat to just until the sugar dissolves. Do not let boil. Stir continuously with a wooden spoon, scraping the bottom of the saucepan to prevent the mixture from scorching. Take it off the heat and cool by placing the saucepan in a large bowl of ice water.

When the gelatin mixture begins to thicken, pour it on top of the diced fruit in the molds, gather the plastic wrap to create small bundles and refrigerate until the gelatin sets.

Turn out the fruit jellies, gently remove the plastic wrap, and serve, either wrapped in bamboo-leaf cups or placed directly in attractive glass dishes.

How to make a perfect cup of green tea

In Japan, tea is consumed all day, from breakfast in the morning to dinner in the evening. If you go to any business meeting, you will be automatically presented with a cup of tea. All hotel rooms in Japan are equipped with tea-making equipment. In a restaurant, your tea cup will be constantly refilled. It is inconceivable to have a meal without tea. In other words, tea is drunk all the time, everywhere.

Freshly picked tea leaves are immediately steamed to prevent discoloration and fermentation, then dried by rolling and crumbling and finally by hot air. The color, aroma, and shape of the leaves define the quality of the tea. Japanese green tea should not be brewed with boiling-hot water, and the better the quality of tea, the lower the temperature of the water used. Here I have listed five varieties of tea enjoyed with or without a meal.

Freshly picked tea leaves are immediately steamed to prevent discoloration and fermentation, then dried by rolling and crumbling and finally by hot air. The color, aroma, and shape of the leaves define the quality of the tea. Japanese green tea should not be brewed with boiling-hot water, and the better the quality of tea, the lower the temperature of the water used. Here I have listed five varieties of tea enjoyed with or without a meal.

Gyokuro

Its name meaning "jewel dew," this is the highest-quality tea made from young tender leaves picked in early spring. The tea leaves are highly fragrant and a deep shiny green. The tea should be brewed in small amounts in warm water about 122°F. It is drunk on its own or accompanied with *wagashi* (Japanese candies), but not with a meal. Brew it for no more than 2–3 minutes.

Sencha

This literally means "infused tea". It is a middle-ranking, good everyday tea drunk at home. The tea should be brewed in water about 140°F. Used tea leaves can be reused for a second time, using slightly hotter water.

Bancha

This is an everyday, ordinary drinking tea served freely in restaurants and offices. It is made of larger leaves and stems and makes a yellowish green tea. There are varying qualities of bancha and, the lower the grade, the more stems and even twigs are included.

Hojicha

This is a roasted bancha with a nutty, woody flavor. It is the tea most often drunk with a meal, especially breakfast.

sauces and dressings

A good friend of mine who was then a head chef of a famous Japanese restaurant in London winked and told me once that "it is all in the sauce", as he applied professional finishing touches to my dish. Indeed there were more than two dozen sauces and dressings on a large tray, all ready to be used in plastic squeeze bottles. I watched him selecting one as if he were an artist carefully choosing paint.

Sauces and dressings are essentially a way of adding more flavor and sometimes an additional texture. They provide another layer, giving a dish extra depth and character. I have always regarded sauces, marinades, and dressings rather like accessories, making sometimes dramatic and at other times subtle changes to a simple black dress. Of course, a home cook is not expected to compete with professionals, but a few carefully selected homemade sauces and dressings will

expand your cooking repertoire enormously and help cut down on time spent cooking, so that you can enjoy eating the delicious results with your family and friends. This chapter should be used in tandem with the earlier section on soy sauce, vinegar, miso, sake, and mirin (pages 12–13). In Japanese cooking, those five ingredients provide the platform of basic taste and flavor. Making a sauce is a matter of combining those seasoning ingredients. It is tempting to use everything you like, from soy sauce to sweet mirin or spicy chile, but my advice is to keep it simple—decide which of the basic flavors you wish to build on and do not confuse it by adding too many conflicting seasoning ingredients. As your confidence increases, I am sure that you will soon develop your own sauces and dressings, but here are some recipes to start with.

Teriyaki sauce

After soy sauce, teriyaki must be the most popular and widely used sauce in Japanese cooking. Although it is possible to buy ready made versions, homemade teriyaki is always better, more economical, and healthier because you know what went into it. I always make a large quantity and divide it into four batches, keeping one plain and infusing the others with garlic, chile, and ginger.

5 tablespoons soy sauce

5 tablespoons sake

5 tablespoons mirin

3 tablespoons granulated sugar
  (you may vary the amount to
  suit your taste)

Put all the ingredients in a wide shallow saucepan over a moderate heat and stir to ensure the sugar dissolves. Bring to a boil, then lower the heat to simmer until the sauce has reduced by one quarter. Let it cool completely before storing in the refrigerator in a glass jar with a lid.

To make the garlic-infused sauce, peel a whole clove of garlic, bruise it slightly with the blade of your kitchen knife and place it in the teriyaki sauce while it is still warm. For the chile-infused sauce, make an incision lengthwise in a large red chile (serrano or jalapeño) and then place it in the still-warm sauce. For the ginger-infused sauce, peel a thumb-sized piece of fresh ginger root, bruise it slightly with the blade of your kitchen knife, and put it in the still-warm sauce.

Cook's tip
Teriyaki sauce will keep refrigerated, up to 3 weeks, but its initial nutty aroma will deteriorate with time.

Dashi joyu

This is my most useful sauce of all time—there is always a jar in my refrigerator. I use it as a noodle dipping sauce, marinade, a cooking liquid for rice, or to simply pour over a chilled block of tofu. It is highly versatile. It is not as strongly flavored as pure soy sauce, but more subtle and more flavorsome than ordinary dashi broth.

2 x 2-inch piece of konbu
  (kelp seaweed)

1/2 cup mirin

3 tablespoons sake

1/3 cup soy sauce

1/4 ounce dried bonito flakes

Put a nonstick skillet over a low heat and dry-toast the piece of konbu to enhance its flavor. Put the mirin and sake in a saucepan over a moderate heat and bring to a boil to burn off the alcohol. Add the soy sauce and return to a boil before turning off the heat. Add the dried bonito flakes and set aside to cool. Line a sieve with a paper towel and strain the liquid. Transfer to a storage jar and add the konbu. Let sit 2–3 days at room temperature before using, so the konbu will infuse the sauce with its flavor. Refrigerate any leftovers.

Cook's tip
You can turn this into a refreshing salad dressing by adding grated daikon (Japanese white radish). Or you can make a Japanese barbecue sauce by adding tomato ketchup and grated garlic.

Yunan miso—citrus miso

It is hard to choose one miso-based sauce from endless variations, but I think this recipe is one of the most versatile and has an excellent rich citrus flavor. You can use this recipe as a salad dressing, marinade sauce for steamed vegetables, barbecue sauce, or even as a dip with a difference.

1/3 cup sake

1/3 cup mirin

11 ounces white or light-colored miso paste

1/4 cup light soy sauce

3 tablespoons yuzu juice or lime juice

Put the sake and mirin in a saucepan over high heat. Bring to a boil and cook for 2 minutes to burn off the alcohol. Turn off the heat and add the miso paste little by little, stirring well with a whisk to ensure all the miso is dissolved. Add the soy sauce and yuzu or lime juice and let cool completely before storing in a glass jar.

Cook's tip

This miso mixture works wonderfully as a marinade—try marinating salmon fillets or mackerel overnight with it. (Pat the fish dry with paper towels before cooking.) It also makes an excellent salad dressing: dilute it with, preferably, dashi broth, or just water to preferred consistency.

Sanbaizu—savory sweet vinegar

In Japanese cooking, vinegar plays many important but often hidden roles—it is used to draw out excess moisture and odor, it highlights *umami* and subtly seasons fish or vegetables. For vegetables, vinegar is used to freshen both the texture and color. *Sanbaizu* is one of the three classic vinegar blends, which is flavored with soy sauce and bonito flakes and is mildly sweetened with sugar. It can be used on its own like a salad dressing, as a seasoning for steamed vegetables or served with deep- or shallow-fried food.

1 cup rice vinegar

1/3 cup granulated sugar

5 tablespoons soy sauce

1/4 ounce dried bonito flakes

Combine the vinegar, sugar, and soy sauce in a saucepan. Bring to a boil over a moderate heat. Stir to ensure that all the sugar is dissolved. Turn off the heat, add the bonito fish flakes, and set aside to cool. Line a fine sieve with a paper towel to strain the vinegar mixture. Refrigerate and use within 2 weeks.

Cook's tip

I put a few strips of konbu (kelp seaweed) in the bottle of rice vinegar so the vinegar is naturally infused with the konbu's umami. In the case of teriyaki sauce, use chile or garlic to add extra flavor to the *sanbaizu*.

sweet vinegar miso dressing

5 tablespoons sake

7 ounces white or light-colored
  miso paste

1/3 cup granulated sugar

1/3 cup rice vinegar

Put the sake in a saucepan and bring to a boil over a high heat. Cook 2 minutes to burn off the alcohol. Reduce the heat to moderate/low and add the miso paste, sugar, and vinegar. Cook 5–7 minutes, stirring constantly with a wooden spoon. Turn off the heat when all the ingredients are fully combined and the consistency resembles that of thick yogurt. Let cool, store in a glass jar and refrigerate. The dressing keeps for 4–5 weeks.

Japanese salad dressing

Salads are not in the traditional Japanese repertoire, but to a nation of vegetable lovers salad has become a familiar dish on Japanese tables. The popularity of salads is not hard to understand considering that there are many salad equivalents, such as *sunomono*, vinegar-flavored dishes, and *aemono*, coated vegetables or fish with various sauces such as tofu or miso paste. These small dishes are treated as side dishes either to whet the appetite or cleanse the palate between courses in which many varieties of vinegar-based sauces are used. This recipe is more of a Western salad dressing, but with a Japanese twist.

2 shallots, peeled and grated

3 tablespoons rice vinegar

1 1/2 tablespoons soy sauce

1 1/2 tablespoons sunflower oil

1 teaspoon grainy mustard

1 teaspoon sesame oil

1/2 teaspoon granulated sugar

1/2–1 garlic clove, peeled and
  finely grated

pinch each of salt and pepper

Combine all the ingredients in a lidded glass jar and shake it vigorously to mix. Keep refrigerated and use within 2 days.

Cook's tip

Try making this with grated daikon (Japanese white radish) instead of shallots, adding a few drops of lemon juice for variation.

The art of serving and presentation

Eating a Japanese meal engages all five senses, not just taste and smell, but first of all the appearance of the food, which captures and excites your desire to eat. The presentation of food is an integral part of Japanese cuisine. I have already stressed the importance of the four seasons in Japanese cuisine, but the Japanese sensitivity and appreciation of nature's cycle does not end in choosing seasonal ingredients and cooking them in seasonally appropriate methods; it extends to serving and presentation. We aim to bring the seasons directly to the table.

At the beginning of each season, I used to help my mother change not only the tableware but also our clothes, the paintings and the scrolls hung on the walls, and ornaments in the house. I remember it always being a happy and exciting occasion that made me aware of and appreciate the cycle of the seasons and the rhythms of nature. In Japan, restaurants and traditional inns have at least four sets of tableware and often many more for different seasonal festive occasions. Even private homes have a wide range of tableware in different materials, shapes, colors, and sizes. I am not suggesting that you buy a whole range of Japanese tableware, but you might perhaps acquire one or two Japanese-inspired platters or bowls and mix them with your existing dishes.

At a Japanese home table there is no requirement for uniformity of tableware; rather, the cook is encouraged to mix and match containers fashioned from a variety of materials— pottery, porcelain, glass, lacquer, wood, or bamboo. I also borrow bits of nature—flowers and leaves from the garden, driftwood, pebbles and shells from the beach, red berries, and acorns; all these bring a seasonal touch to the table. But remember that the Japanese way is: "less is more."

Serving suggestions

A home cook has to work within the limits of his or her existing tableware, but keeping within these confines often makes you more innovative—it is perfectly possible to create different effects with a single round dinner plate. For example, do not fill the whole plate with food but leave a large area of it uncovered. The art of serving Japanese food

lies in the ability to reflect nature on the plate. You paint a culinary landscape—there is a mountain, a small mound of food and at the foot there is the sea, the cooking liquid or a sauce, and then the sky depicted by the uncovered parts of the plate. The same principle of creating a landscape applies to serving soups.

You can achieve a harmonious balance on the plate by using the principle of five colors (see page 8) that not only results in a nutritiously balanced dish but also provides contrasting colors. Do not put the same-colored vegetables next to each other. The principle also applies to shapes of food—generally, round-shaped food such as rolled sushi or rolled meat looks more interesting if served on square or rectangular plates. If you do not possess different-shaped plates, it is possible to create the shape on a round plate by using a sheet of nori, or a banana leaf, or by drawing a square line with the sauce.

Another serving principle is number—the Japanese prefer odd numbers like three and five, because it is easier to create contrasts with odd numbers than with even numbers. We particularly shy away from four, as the sound of the number, *shi,* is the same as the word for death and we consider it ominous. Do not serve four pieces or slices of any Japanese food. And you don't always have to serve individually— presenting food on a big platter is a practical and dramatic way of serving that never fails to impress your guests. It also allows people to decide how much they wish to take.

The garnish is important; there is a saying in Japan that just as a person can't go out naked, neither can food. Carefully placed shiso leaves or a small sprig of shiso flowers or wasabi paste molded in a leaf are integral to the art of presentation. In Japan, there is a wide variety of edible garnishes on sale, from leaves to flowers and berries. In the West, we have to be imaginative and use substitutes—sprigs of herbs, cress, or halved cherry tomatoes are a good start. I use dandelion flowers in the spring, strawberry flowers in the summer, and non-toxic leaves in the autumn.

The art of presentation and serving is to bring out the best of food you cooked so that it gives maximum enjoyment to your family and friends.

Etiquette

In the relaxed atmosphere of the home, either at a family meal or even at a dinner party with friends, there is no need to observe strict etiquette or formal table manners other than the most obvious show of appreciation for the food. However, knowing a few basic do's and don'ts of Japanese dining etiquette will help you relax and ultimately increase the pleasure of eating. So here I have listed some of the essentials, mainly regarding chopsticks.

At the start of a Japanese meal we have the Japanese equivalent of grace – we put our hands together in front of our faces, look at the table and say, "*Itadakimasu,*" I receive with gratitude. This one word says it all. You don't have to be fluent in Japanese but take a brief moment, with your hands together or not, to first look at the food placed before you and engage your visual sense. Next, breathe in the aromas and contemplate the pleasures you are about to experience. It doesn't have to be long, just a minute, or even a few seconds, but taking a moment before you begin eating prepares you to engage all your senses and truly appreciate the food you are about to receive; it is a gift of nourishment and good health.

If you are given a pair of disposable wooden chopsticks in a paper sleeve, take them out of the sleeve, carefully break them apart and rest them on the small chopstick rest placed in front of you. The same pair is used throughout the meal. Do not wave them around, point at things, or chew on the end. If there is no rest, when you are not using the chopsticks you should lay them parallel to the edge of the table in front of you. Keeping a pair of chopsticks neatly closed together is rather like sitting properly with your legs together. It certainly makes me feel uncomfortable to see a pair of chopsticks strewn carelessly on the table. When there is no chopstick rest you can have a fun by making an origami one with the paper sleeve.

Never stick chopsticks upright into a bowl of rice—it reminds superstitious Japanese of the incense stands at traditional Japanese funerals. You should also never pass a piece of food to another with your chopsticks because not only is it not hygienic, it's again reminiscent of the Japanese funeral ceremony. If rice is served in a bowl, pick up the bowl with your left hand and hold it close to eat, but don't put your lips to it. And by the way, never ever pour soy sauce on your rice—keep it clean and unadulterated.

If you are helping yourself from a large communal plate or serving someone else, it is hygienic and considered polite to turn your chopsticks around and use the top ends.

At the end of a meal, place the chopsticks you have been using neatly in front of you—this shows that you are satisfied and nourished by the meal you just had.

The Japanese equivalent of grace at the end of a meal is "*Gochisosama*", I have received with gratitude. Again we say this one word with our hands held together in front of us, with our heads slightly bowed.

If all this chopstick etiquette sound too much for you, here is one easy rule to remember—hold your cup or glass when someone pours you a drink and return the courtesy by pouring a drink in turn.

It is alright to slurp when you are eating a bowl of noodles in broth—it is considered a sign of appreciation. But never slurp when eating soup.

Composing a Japanese menu

Principles and examples When devising a menu, I try to chart the basic guidelines, which can be followed by drawing on good old common sense. Courses served side by side should not compete, but complement each other and work harmoniously to provide a balanced meal. The same principle applies to the texture of courses—no one is likely to enjoy a sequence of courses that are equally runny, or dense, or starchy.

So always try to provide a harmonious balance in tastes and texture. My practical advice is to start with cooking just one course or single dish from this book and incorporate it into your existing repertoire, rather than embarking on an ambitious full Japanese three-course menu. And as you gain more confidence in cooking Japanese dishes, gradually expand. It is always better

Spring lunch party
Japanese omelet with tomato and chives
Smoked salmon, salmon roe, and grated daikon noodle salad
Broccoli and scrambled egg sushi

Summer barbecue
Asian gazpacho
Japanese-style chicken burgers
Chicken teriyaki
Spicy edamame and/or grilled corn with teriyaki sauce
Green salad with Japanese salad dressing

Rustic autumn family supper
Autumn mushroom soup
Simmered sardines in ginger vinegar/Slow-cooked belly of pork
Shimeji mushroom and chicken rice

Winter warming dinner
Hokkaido salmon and potato miso soup
Pan sautéed marlin with citrus miso teriyaki sauce
Pan-roasted rack of lamb with rice vinegar/

Sake steamed chicken parcels with pak choi
Warm bean sprout salad with crispy garlic
Dorayaki

Fish feast
New sashimi of sea bream with hot oil
Oyster soupy rice
Wakame and yam salad
Green tea ice cream with adzuki bean paste

Vegetarian lunch
Japanese spring cabbage coleslaw
Japanese new potato salad with tofu mayonnaise
Warm tofu and steamed vegetable salad
Hijiki pasta

Vegetarian dinner
Spring vegetable minestrone soup with white miso
Zen tofu hotpot
Purple sprouting broccoli with mustard soy

Elegant ladies' lunch
Porgy in clear dashi soup
Cucumber and steamed chicken salad with sesame and
  miso dressing
Chilled tomato somen

Celebration dinner
Smoked salmon, salmon roe and caper sushi
Chicken hotpot
Daikon salad with watercress and walnuts

Romantic supper for two
Vine-ripened tomato in red miso with coriander pesto
Japanese-style beef steak
Asparagus and fava bean domburi

Index

Acknowledgements

My big thank you goes to the team that created this book. The very first thank you to Kyle Cathie for commissioning, support and advise to make this possible—I thank you for giving me so much room and trust, you are my guiding inspiration. My editor Sophie Allen for her calm and tireless work in project managing and editing—you made everything seems so easy. To Vanessa Courtier for her long hours behind the scenes in designing. Linda Tubby for interpreting my recipes and preparing flawless food. Louise Mackaness, home economist for preparing and styling the food for the front cover. Wei Tang, stylist for her fine choices. Jan Baldwin for taking such beautiful and inviting photos—you are such a sympathetic photographer and made me feel at ease in front of the camera instead of wanting to run away from it.

A huge gratitude goes to my family, my husband Stephen, our three boys, Maxi, Frederick, and Dominic, for their patience, understanding and support while I worked many weekends and their willingness to test many new recipes.

Arigato to Mrs. Junko Ohotaki for her enthusiastic support, to her young doctor son, Yuhei for his fine calligraphy and most of all, their warmest friendship. Another big *arigato* goes to Mrs. Rie Tada and her late husband.

A big thank you to Rosie and Eric Treuile at London's Mecca for foodies, Books for Cooks, for giving me the initial opportunity for starting my food career and your continued support.